UNDERCOVER FIGHTERS

THE BRITISH 22nd SAS REGIMENT

D0964883

VILLARD MILITARY SERIES

UNDERCOVER FIGHTERS

THE BRITISH 22nd SAS REGIMENT

Series Editor: Ashley Brown

Consultant Editors:

**Brigadier-General
James L Collins Jr (Retd)**

Dr John Pimlott

**Brigadier-General
Edwin H Simmons USMC (Retd)**

VILLARD BOOKS NEW YORK

1986

First published in Great Britain by Orbis Publishing Limited, London

Contributing Authors

Max Arthur
Brigadier Michael Calvert
Captain Derrick Harrison
Jonathan Reed
Major-General John Strawson
Paul Szuscikiewicz
Francis Toase
Ian Westwell

Acknowledgments

Photographs were supplied by:
Lieutenant-General J.B. Akehurst CBE, Brigadier Michael Calvert, Camera Press, John Cooper, *Daily Telegraph* Colour Library, Tony Geraghty, Captain Harrison, Imperial War Museum, Major M.J. Kealy, London Express News and Features Service, Hugh McManners, Photographers International, Popperfoto, Press Association, Rex Features, SAS Regimental Association, *Soldier* Magazine, Frank Spooner Pictures.

The publishers would like to thank the SAS Regimental Association, and also Lieutenant-Colonel John Cooper, Bob Bennett and Reg Seekings for their help in preparing this book.

Front cover photograph: SAS Trooper in Borneo (Daily Telegraph Colour Library)
Back cover photograph: SAS men on exercise (Photographers International)
Title spread: SAS Trooper, Falklands 1982

Library of Congress Catalog Card Number: 85-40983
ISBN: 0-394-74405-5

Printed in Italy
9 8 7 6 5 4 3 2
First Edition

CONTENTS

INTRODUCTION
The SAS in World War II

Below: David Stirling (standing) photographed with members of a raiding party shortly before his capture in Tunisia. Stirling's unorthodox and flexible approach to the desert war achieved many dramatic successes, and, with only a handful of men, he was able to inflict serious damage on the Axis war effort in North Africa. From July 1942 the SAS made great use of heavily armed, four-wheel-drive jeeps, and on many occasions would shoot their way in and out of trouble with all guns blazing.

IN JULY 1941 North Africa was the main scene of British combat operations against the German Army. A British force based in Egypt confronted German and Italian troops defending the Italian colony of Libya. The Western Desert (as this area was known to the British) was a hostile environment in which to wage war. Roads were poor along the coast and almost nonexistent in the hinterland. Armies, heavily dependent upon their lines of supply, rely on a variety of installations – vehicle parks, POL (petrol, oil, lubricants) dumps, airfields and staff headquarters – to ensure the maintenance of their fighting power. In the Western Desert these installations were largely concentrated along the coast, near the ports where supplies would arrive from Europe. As an army moved further from its main port, so its supply line became more tenuous and more vulnerable.

David Stirling, a Scots Guards lieutenant, had participated in a number of large-scale raids on communications targets along the Cyrenaican coast. These had all ended in failure, as the size of the force made their presence in the vicinity of

he target easily detectable. These unsuccessful ventures nagged at Stirling and he started thinking about alternative methods of raiding that might be employed.

Stirling concluded that the concept of raids against enemy 'soft' targets was still sound, but that the forces hitherto used were too large and cumbersome to achieve the surprise necessary for a successful attack. He proposed that a small unit of four or five men could successfully infiltrate enemy lines and strike at lightly defended targets. Their usefulness could be increased by making these men extremely versatile fighters, able to reach their targets by sea, land or parachute. His ideas were soon brought to the attention of the commanders of the British Middle East Forces, General Sir Claude Auchinleck and Major-General Sir Neil Ritchie. They gave Stirling permission to implement his ideas, placing him in charge of the SAS's operational planning and training. The SAS began as 'L' Detachment, Special Air Service Brigade – a name chosen to deceive German intelligence into thinking that a whole new airborne brigade had been formed – and its 65 members set up their training camp at Kabrit on the Suez Canal.

The first SAS raids were launched against the airfields at Timimi and Gazala on 16 November 1941. The men were to

In late 1940 a commando brigade, known as Layforce, was dispatched to North Africa to carry out raids against the Italian Army. By mid-1941, however, Layforce had been severely mauled and was earmarked for disbandment. At this stage, David Stirling, a Scots Guards subaltern in No.8 Commando, received permission to recruit a small force for raids deep behind enemy lines.

Some 65 men, drawn from Layforce and known as 'L' Detachment, assembled at Kabrit on the Suez Canal for para training. The first jump, on 16 November, was a total disaster with the detachment, losing nearly 70 per cent of its strength. Stirling immediately abandoned the para concept and opted to use the Long Range Desert Group to get his men to and from their targets. Success was almost immediate and Stirling, by this time a major, was allowed to expand his force. New recruits flocked in: 50 French paras, later known as the French Squadron SAS; men from the Special Boat Squadron (SBS); in March, the Greek Sacred Squadron; in June, the Special Interrogation Group of anti-Nazi Germans; and in August, more SBS men. By January 1943, Stirling's force had grown to regimental size and was renamed 1 SAS. Total strength was around 750 men.

The successes of 1 SAS did not go unnoticed and David Stirling's brother, William, was allowed to form 2 SAS from men of 62 Commando, but the new regiment was only officially inaugurated in May 1943.

In early 1943 David Stirling was captured in Tunisia and command of 1 SAS passed to Paddy Mayne who led the regiment until the end of the desert campaign in May.

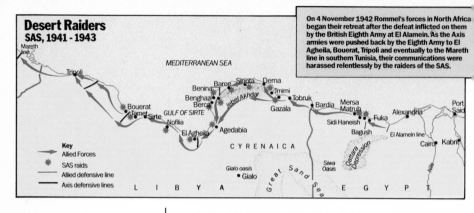

Desert Raiders
SAS, 1941 - 1943

On 4 November 1942 Rommel's forces in North Africa began their retreat after the defeat inflicted on them by the British Eighth Army at El Alamein. As the Axis armies were pushed back by the Eighth Army to El Agheila, Bouerat, Tripoli and eventually to the Mareth line in southern Tunisia, their communications were harassed relentlessly by the raiders of the SAS.

MEDITERRANEAN SEA

Key
- Allied Forces
- SAS raids
- Allied defensive line
- Axis defensive lines

Below: During parachute training at Kabrit, the first SAS camp, Bob Bennett leaps from a scaffolding tower. Every SAS man was expected to earn his parachute wings.

Far right: Lieutenant Edward McDonald is dressed in shorts, bush jacket and an Arab *shemagh*. Leather gauntlets and Arab sandals are also worn, and McDonald carries a Sykes-Fairbairn commando dagger on his belt.

be dropped by parachute from bombers and make their way to their targets overland. Unfortunately, these two initial operations were failures because weather conditions were totally unsuitable for parachute drops. The raids bore fruit of another kind, however. After landing, some of the SAS parties managed to make their way to their rendezvous with the Long Range Desert Group (LRDG) which was to drive them back to base. Here Stirling met David Lloyd Owen of the LRDG, who suggested that his men should be used to drive the SAS to its targets. The result was that on a second pair of raids, conducted in December, two SAS groups succeeded in destroying a total of 61 enemy aircraft.

Throughout 1942, the SAS raided enemy airfields, supply dumps and shipping in harbours. Mobility was improved by the acquisition of a number of jeeps, which were heavily armed with Browning .50 calibre and Vickers K machine guns. During the Bagush raid on the night of 7 July 1942, these jeeps were put to good effect when they charged across the airfield, shooting up the enemy aircraft with their machine guns.

After the defeat of Rommel's forces at El Alamein in November 1942, the SAS concentrated its efforts against the roads used by the German and Italian forces in retreat. It successfully forced some enemy traffic off the roads during the night, thereby complementing the RAF's ground-attack aircraft which harried daytime movements. Once Anglo-American forces had landed in the French North African colonies (Operation Torch), German and Italian forces moved into Tunisia, where they occupied defensive positions prepared by the French in case of an Italian attack from Libya. Once again the SAS went into action against the enemy's supply lines. However, the Tunisian countryside was not as suitable for its operations as Libya had been. The flattish desert wastes of the Libyan interior were replaced by the scrub-covered Tunisian hills and cultivated valleys. The population was also less sympathetic than the Libyans to an Allied victory. The result of these factors was that the SAS had a rather mixed record of operations. Many members of the Regiment were captured, including the commander and

By early 1942 the future of the SAS seemed assured and, despite some official hostility, David Stirling set about devising a badge for the unit. The colours of the new insignia were dark and light blue, reflecting the Oxford and Cambridge rowing background of two SAS officers.

Originally, the cap badge was to be a flaming Sword of Damocles with the motto 'Who Dares Wins', but a local tailor produced a design more reminiscent of a winged dagger (above). Parachute wings in white with two shades of blue were also produced. Worn on the upper arm they were presented after seven jumps. Men who performed with particular gallantry were permitted to wear the wings on their left breast. The cap badge was worn on many different types of headgear, but a beige beret was the norm.

Following the Axis surrender in North Africa in May 1943, the future of the SAS was again in doubt. 1 SAS was actually disbanded for a short time.

The decision to invade Sicily, however, meant that the special skills of the SAS were once again in demand, and 1 SAS was renamed the Special Raiding Squadron, led by Paddy Mayne, while 2 SAS under William Stirling continued as before. The SRS and 2 SAS operated in advance of the main Allied landing in Sicily in July 1943, and then behind enemy lines. Soon afterwards it was decided to use the SRS in the coming invasion of northwest Europe. Reverting to their old title of 1 SAS, the SRS returned to the UK, where they were joined by elements of 2 SAS early in 1944.

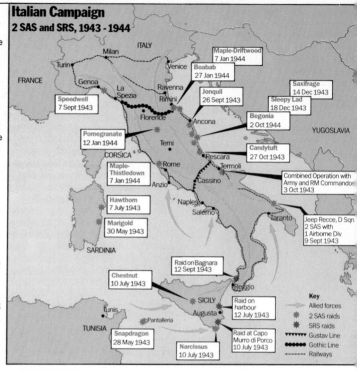

Italian Campaign
2 SAS and SRS, 1943 - 1944

Maple-Driftwood 7 Jan 1944
Boabab 27 Jan 1944
Saxifrage 14 Dec 1943
Sleepy Lad 18 Dec 1943
Jonquil 26 Sept 1943
Speedwell 7 Sept 1943
Begonia 2 Oct 1944
Pomegranate 12 Jan 1944
Candytuft 27 Oct 1943
Maple-Thistledown 7 Jan 1944
Combined Operation with Army and RM Commandos 3 Oct 1943
Hawthorn 7 July 1943
Marigold 30 May 1943
Jeep Recce, D Sqn 2 SAS with 1 Airborne Div 9 Sept 1943
Raid on Bagnara 12 Sept 1943
Chestnut 10 July 1943
SICILY
Raid on harbour 12 July 1943
Snapdragon 28 May 1943
Raid at Capo Murro di Porco 10 July 1943
Narcissus 10 July 1943

Key
→ Allied forces
✳ 2 SAS raids
✳ SRS raids
▾▾▾▾ Gustav Line
●●●● Gothic Line
······ Railways

THE SAS IN EUROPE

Having returned to Great Britain to prepare for the invasion of northwest Europe, 1 and 2 SAS were brigaded together, under the command of Brigadier Roderick McLeod, as part of the 1st Airborne Division, and joined by 3 and 4 SAS (French troops) and a Belgian squadron (later 5 SAS).

In the four months following D-day in June 1944, some 2000 SAS men were deployed across the length and breadth of occupied France and the Low Countries. They operated in uniform from more than 40 secret bases up to 250 miles behind enemy lines, and helped in gathering intelligence and disrupting communications.

In February 1945, McLeod was replaced by Major Michael Calvert, a former Chindit leader with great experience of unconventional warfare. As the Allies moved further into northwest Europe (and especially after the crossing of the Rhine in March 1945), SAS squadrons, working independently or with armoured units, raced across north Europe, protecting the flanks of advancing friendly units.

The last big operation of the wartime SAS was the collection and repatriation of the German forces in Norway. After this, the brigade was broken up. The Belgians and French returned to their own national armies, while 1 and 2 SAS were disbanded in October 1945. During the campaign in northwest Europe, the SAS had killed or wounded some 8000 enemy troops, at a cost of 350 casualties.

founder, David Stirling. Their nuisance value is reflected, however, by the fact that the Germans thought it necessary to form a special company to hunt down SAS raiding parties..

After the surrender of the Axis forces in Tunisia, the North African campaign came to an end and the SAS underwent a complete reorganisation. A second SAS regiment, made up of men from 62 Commando, began to train at Philippeville in Algeria, and was officially established in May 1943, while 1 SAS was reformed as the Special Raiding Squadron (SRS). This unit was to attack German and Italian coastal positions in the Balkans and central Mediterranean. During the invasion of Sicily in July 1943, the SRS successfully assaulted a number of coastal positions, while some members of 2 SAS were dropped by parachute behind enemy lines in support of the Allied landings to perform their usual duties of raiding supply routes. 2 SAS, led by David Stirling's brother William, also participated in the Italian campaign, and was given free licence to operate against the enemy's supply lines. His men struck at vulnerable points behind the front line, destroying bridges, hitting airfields and coordinating the efforts of partisan groups. In many cases, small teams were put in by parachute, harrying the Germans for several weeks before returning to the Allied lines.

While the SAS was active in the Mediterranean theatre, preparations were also being made for its role in the invasion of France. As well as raiding enemy communications, David Stirling had also envisaged that the SAS could act in conjunction with Resistance forces operating behind enemy lines. The highly trained SAS men would provide a nucleus of disciplined troops to organise the Resistance groups into units capable of coordinated action against enemy soldiers in their area.

Most SAS operations in the liberation of France were conducted along these lines. Operation Kipling, which took place between 14 August and 25 September 1944 to the west of Auxerre in central France, is a good example of the 40 or so operations that took place that summer and autumn. The initial phase was carried out by six men of 1 SAS, ordered to

Captain Derrick Harrison (above, second from right) volunteered for the army on the day Germany marched into Poland. In 1940 he was commissioned into the Cheshire Regiment and served in England with the 4th Battalion. He then transferred and went to the Middle East with the 6th Battalion as part of the 44th (Home Counties) Division for the Alamein offensive and later became 2 IC, Mobile Troops, Base Camp, Geneifa on the Suez Canal. To escape this task he volunteered, unsuccessfully, for both the Sudan Defence Force and the British-officered Jebel Druze in Lebanon. Eventually, hearing of 'a mysterious, secret unit' he walked into the SAS camp at Kabrit, was interviewed by the legendary Paddy Mayne, and was accepted. He took part in the SRS actions in Sicily and Italy, parachuted into France in August 1944 (Operations Kipling and Houndsworth), worked in support of Corps Field Security, Holland, in the winter of 1944–45, and operated with the SAS ahead of the Canadian armour in Germany.

Left: Two SAS men with a .303in Vickers machine gun in Italy.

An original member of 'L' Detachment, Bob Bennett, BEM, MM (above) was with 1 SAS for most of World War II. At the outbreak of the conflict, he was in the Brigade of Guards, but soon joined No. 8 Commando. In mid-1941 Bennett transferred to the SAS and fought throughout the desert campaign. During the latter stages of the war he served in Italy, northwest Germany, and Norway. After the SAS was disbanded in 1945, he joined the Allied Screening Commission and was a military advisor to the Greeks during the Greek Civil War until 1949.

After a spell in civvies and a time with the Royal Artillery, he began training men of K Squadron, earmarked for the Korean War. In January 1951 he was sent to Malaya where he served with B Squadron, Malayan Scouts (SAS) until 1953.

Returning to the UK he was put in charge of the tough selection programme for men wanting to join the SAS. Between 1955 and 1962, when he left the army, Bennett was the regimental sergeant-major of 21 SAS.

reconnoitre the area and to assess its suitability for the deployment of C Squadron, 1 SAS. Captain Derrick Harrison, commander of the team, decided to send for more men. After three nights of parachute drops, Captain Harrison had 27 men and five jeeps at his disposal. He began operations, ambushing German patrols and convoys. Intelligence proved somewhat erratic, and on one occasion a 'convoy' turned out to be a solitary German soldier. The lack of accurate maps also caused problems.

A drive to Aillant to repair a damaged jeep led to Operation Kipling's major action. Captain Harrison recalls:

'As we reached the road we saw an ominous pillar of smoke rising into the air over in the direction of Les Ormes. We headed towards it at speed.'

'I opened up with my machine guns and saw some of the Germans fall'

It soon became clear from the sound of firing that there was a group of Germans in the village, possibly engaged in a firefight with the Maquis [Resistance], Captain Harrison, with five men and two jeeps, decided that a surprise attack was called for:

'The Union Jacks on our jeeps jerked into life as we accelerated into the village square. In the road stood a large German truck and two staff cars, blocking the way through. A crowd of SS men in front of the church dashed for cover as I opened up with my machine guns and, as the vehicles burst into flames, I saw some of the Germans fall. But now I was in trouble. My jeep had come to a sudden halt, my Vickers K jammed and the Germans were firing back.'

Captain Harrison's driver, 'Curly' Hall, had been shot. Harrison grabbed his carbine and began to return the fire of the seemingly innumerable Germans around him.

'Suddenly, my right hand was warm, wet and slippery – blood. I had been hit. This posed another difficulty: how to change magazines? Somehow, in a fumbling manner, I managed. Then I heard Stewart Richardson shout a warning: "To your left! The orchard!" I moved to the left and saw some 20 men moving through the small, walled orchard towards me. Fire! Change mag. Fire! Slowly they fell back, leaving some of their number dead or wounded.

'Now I saw that Fauchois, one of Richardson's crew, had dashed forward in an attempt to retrieve Hall's body. I yelled to him to get back, as the Germans concentrated their fire on him. Brearton, Richardson's driver, was now turning his jeep round, to bring the rear Vickers into action. As I sprinted for the jeep, a head appeared at a window in the house above. Without hesitation, Richardson raised his Colt 45 and dropped the German with one shot. With a scream of tyres and a final burst from the Vickers we left the scene.'

Captain Harrison and his men had interrupted the execution of 20 hostages by the SS. The hostages had managed to

Left: An officer of 1 SAS in
Germany, 1945. He wears his SAS
badge on a paratrooper's red
beret. The 1937-pattern webbing
pouches hold a compass and
ammunition for the revolver. He
also wears a 'Denison' smock,
dispatch rider's breeches and
motorcycle boots.
Above: An SAS jeep in France in
1944. On the left is Corporal
Duffy, who was captured in
August, and then escaped from a
hospital near Fontainebleau dressed
as a German medical officer.

Above: A jeep from D Squadron arrives at Kiel harbour in early May 1945. The Willys jeeps used by the SAS in Europe were fitted with armour-plate shields and bullet-proof glass to protect the driver and front gunner. Armament usually consisted of a combination of Vickers K (often mounted in pairs) and Browning machine guns. Extra fuel tanks were used to give the jeep a range of over 500 miles. During the advance on Kiel, known as Operation Archway, the SAS ranged ahead of British armour and infantry as a scouting force.

escape in the confusion, while the Nazis had lost some 60 dead and wounded, plus their transport.

Once the Germans had been driven from France, the Allies began to prepare for the crossing of the Rhine and the final defeat of the German armies on their own soil. The SAS was in the forefront of the Allied drive across the Rhine and over the North German Plain. Operation Archway was conducted by 1 SAS with the aim of reconnaissance and engaging in long-range penetration raids. Four squadrons participated, each with about 100 men and 26 jeeps.

Advancing towards Hanover, D Squadron quickly settled into a routine: moving by day, sorting out any opposition, and resting up by night. It was a gruelling and often dangerous regime, with the squadron operating anything up to 70 miles in advance of the Allied armies. Despite meeting the odd pocket of resistance, the men of the SAS kept up the momentum of their advance. D Squadron reached Hanover in early April. As Sergeant Bob Bennett recalled:

'They were very good with their 88s. Several times we had a smoke shell exploding directly above our heads. They were using them to find the range. We got the message loud and clear, and you never saw jeeps move so fast. If an 88 opened up, the driver would throw the jeep into reverse and go like the clappers to get out of range or under cover.'

After reaching Hanover, the SAS began a drive on the Bay of Lubeck. Resistance was now virtually nonexistent and the men concentrated on disarming German civilians and accepting the surrender of enemy troops. After dealing with the enemy near Lubeck at the end of April, 1 SAS was ordered to strike out for the port of Kiel, and reached the city on 3 May 1945. There was no resistance.

After returning to Britain, the SAS was sent to Norway to disarm and repatriate the German troops there. This job lasted for five months. In October 1945, after their return to Britain, 1 and 2 SAS were disbanded. However, this was not the end of the SAS. In the early 1950s the Regiment was re-formed, to fight another war in another part of the world.

1

BEATING
THE BANDITS
The Malayan Emergency

The SAS of World War II was disbanded in October 1945, and its immediate successor was a Territorial Army unit, the 21st SAS Regiment, which was formed in 1947 and known as the 'Artists' Rifles', a famous volunteer unit formed in 1860.
The real heirs to the SAS fighting tradition, however, were the Malayan Scouts. This unit, formed in 1950 for jungle patrolling in Malaya, was part of Malaya Command (whose badge is shown above). The Scouts were led by Major Michael Calvert, former commander of the SAS brigade in northwest Europe. Communist insurgents had been active in Malaya since 1948, and the Scouts were one of the units formed to track them down. Calvert raised 100 men to form A Squadron; members of 21 SAS in London became B Squadron, and Rhodesians recruited by Calvert became C Squadron. In 1952 the Malayan Scouts were fundamentally rearranged, and became the present-day 22nd SAS Regiment.

IN 1953, the CO of 22 SAS, Lieutenant-Colonel Oliver Brooke, arranged a meeting with Major Johnny Cooper of B Squadron. Cooper, an SAS stalwart from the old days and David Stirling's driver in the desert, was instructed to raise a new squadron to fill the gap created by the recent departure home of the Rhodesian Squadron. The sudden loss of a third of the regiment's operational strength in Malaya would, unless replacements could be found, compromise the SAS's ability to carry out long-term deep-penetration missions against the communist terrorists (CTs) holding up in the peninsula's mountainous and jungle-covered interior.

After a few weeks of intensive activity, Cooper had gathered together about 100 men to form D Squadron. Only one officer, Lieutenant Bruce-Murray, and 20 men had had any jungle experience; the rest were fitters from the workshops and medical staff – completely and utterly untried against the CTs. However, Cooper had every faith in his men; a faith that was soon justified:

'On one occasion, a man came staggering into our camp and reported that two of my boys, Corporal "Digger" Bancroft and Trooper Wilkins had been killed by bandits on the other side of a nearby mountain. Bill Speakman, a Korean [War] VC, was with me. He had passed his selection in Malaya and was on his jungle training course before going to Changi to get some jump practice.

'We contacted No. 848 Squadron, the naval unit that had done our parachute drops, and they said that a chopper would be sent to bring out our dead. It was about 1000 hours. I organised a ten-man party, including Bill, to bring the casualties out.

'At about last light, I saw the huge figure of Bill moving down the lower slope of the mountain. He came down and dropped the body of Bancroft at the side of the helicopter. Bill's feet were cut to ribbons but he just turned round and said, "Sir, I'm going straight back." At about 1100 hours on the following morning he returned with the other body. His feet were worse, but he refused to be casevaced [evacuated as a casualty]. He was typical of the sort of chaps I had in the squadron.'

It was vital to carry out deep raids against the enemy's bases

By the mid-1950s, the British strategy in Malaya of denying the CTs the food and intelligence that up until then had been provided by the Chinese squatters in the villages, and harassing the bandits in the jungle fringes, was beginning to pay dividends. The guerrillas had been forced onto the defensive and many groups had retired to the relative safety of the deep jungle. However, if the Emergency was to be brought to a successful conclusion, it was vital that the security forces carry out deep raids against the enemy's bases and deny them the support they enjoyed from the indigenous tribes.

The men of 22 SAS worked in conjunction with the civil and

military authorities, but the scale and scope of their operations were entirely different. Unlike the line regiments who worked on the edges of the plantations for periods of up to four days, the SAS penetrated deep into the primary jungle on assignments that could last up to three months. Regular units usually operated in groups of platoon strength whereas four-man patrols were the norm for the SAS, After a stint in the jungle, the men would have a month off: two weeks' leave and two weeks' retraining to keep them in shape.

As the threat of guerrilla attacks in southern Malaya gradually receded, the SAS was increasingly involved in the pacification of the region around the Cameron Highlands, primarily in a large area of Pahang bordering on the state of Kelantan, and along the frontier with Thailand. The local CTs maintained their headquarters in the highlands and were

Page 15: An SAS patrol clambers from a Whirlwind helicopter hovering over a jungle clearing in Malaya.
Below: A four-man Malayan Scouts patrol poses for the camera. Some members of A Squadron were lacking in discipline and gave the unit a bad name. The job had to be done, however, and the unit had to make do with those who were available and willing.

Above: Major Mike Calvert's experience of jungle warfare during World War II made him the ideal choice to lead the Malayan Scouts, precursors of the postwar SAS.

Below: Fort Brook, one of a number of jungle forts constructed by the SAS in Malaya as centres for the distribution of food and medical supplies to the indigenous tribes. The forts also enabled the SAS to carry the war to the enemy deep in the jungle.

forcing the tribal peoples to provide them with food and information regarding the security forces. The SAS's role was to gather the natives in protected villages and carry the war to the enemy.

The decision to deploy the SAS in a particular area was taken at the very highest level, during the regular meetings of a joint civil, military and police body known as Paragon Control. Representatives of each state would 'bid' for the services of a squadron, basing their request on available intelligence. Once general agreement was reached, the CO of the SAS and his operations officer would give a full briefing to the relevant squadron commander. Cooper attended many pre-deployment meetings and was well aware of the SAS's role:

'The CO would explain the area of operation and provide details of CT activity. The idea was that we would harass the CTs, and establish protected settlements for the Aborigines [indigenous tribes]. As part of the overall "hearts and minds" programme, we had to wean the natives away from the bandits by providing food, accommodation and medical assistance. By building jungle forts, we could protect the natives from CT intimidation. Our first area of deployment was on the Sangrei Brok; the camp was known as Fort Brook.'

As the fort was being built and the adjacent areas cleared for cultivation, more and more natives began to leave their villages for the shelter of the encampment. Many were so terrified of CT reprisals that they refused to divulge any information to the security forces, but a few were willing to guide SAS patrols. With the aid of their local knowledge and

Above: SAS men return from a patrol on Speakman's Hill, named after Bill Speakman, who climbed it twice to recover the bodies of two comrades. Unusually, two of the men of this patrol are carrying the Rifle No.5 (a Lee-Enfield, cut down for jungle operations), in place of the more common M1 carbines. The third man in this patrol carries a Bren light machine gun.

The Malayan Emergency
22 SAS, 1952-1958

THAILAND

• Alor Star

Kota Bahru

SOUTH CHINA SEA

KEDAH

Tanach Merah

PENANG

1952

PERAK

Belum Valley

▲ Anak Reng

Kelantan

KELANTAN

TRENGGANU

Ipoh •

* Beehive (1955)

Termite* Cameron
(1954) Highlands

1958

Telok
Anson

Benta • Kuala Lipis

* Cato (1953)

Bagan
Datoh

Raub

MALAYA

• Kuantan

SELANGOR

PAHANG

Kuala Lumpur •

NEGRI
SEMBILAN

Seremban •

* Hive (1952)

STRAITS

MALACCA Labis • * Eagle
(1953)

OF

MALACCA

JOHORE

Changi

Key

* Major SAS operations
Swamp

Johore Bahru •
Singapore •

The failure of the native Malays and Chinese immigrants to agree on the shape of postwar British administration of the colony provoked the Malayan Communist Party to reform its wartime resistance army. The Malayan Races Liberation Army took to the jungle and conducted a terrorist campaign against British colonial administrators and managers of the country's tin mines and rubber plantations. The British government responded with a counter-insurgency campaign based on the coordination of military and police tactics under civil control. Great emphasis was placed on intelligence-gathering activities and long-range jungle patrolling.

Below: Three SAS patrols return from the jungle. For comfort, the men have taken off their packs, which normally weighed 60-70lb. In line with standard SAS practice, these men have shaved and washed immediately upon emerging from the tropical forest. While on patrol the men normally allowed as much dirt as possible to build up on their bodies, as this discouraged insects from biting. Far right: An SAS patrol moves along a stream through the Malayan jungle. The wide variety of cover available to prospective ambushers made jungle patrolling an extremely nerve-racking activity.

the invaluable help of Sarawak trackers attached to the squadron, Cooper was soon able to report a successful brush with a group of guerrillas:

'We went in on 22 October and stayed for 122 days. During that time we managed to contact members of the Senai tribe but were being continually harassed by the CTs. I sent Bruce-Murray out to patrol the upper reaches of the Sangrei Brok. He was a first-rate jungle operator and managed to suss out a bandit camp. He killed three guerrillas in a very successful two-man operation that got the area started up.'

Once the construction of a fort was nearing completion and the natives had been gathered in, the responsibility for protecting the indigenous tribes passed to the paramilitary forces, often the Police Field Force, and the SAS teams would then carry out long-term deep-penetration raids in pursuit of their elusive enemy. Apart from the odd piece of 'hot' intelligence provided by the locals or the security forces, each squadron was left to its own devices, acting on the initiative of patrol leaders in the field.

Working from the forts, each of a squadron's troops would be allocated an area of jungle to patrol. To prevent friendly

The 22nd SAS Regiment, formed in 1952 out of the Malayan Scouts, soon proved one of the most effective elements of the security forces deployed against the communist insurgents. By 1956, 22 SAS had a strength of 560 men and officers, consisting of A, B and D Squadrons; in addition, in place of the Rhodesian members of the Malayan Scouts who had returned home there was a New Zealand (NZ) Squadron and a short-lived Para Squadron formed from the Parachute Regiment. The SAS took the offensive against the insurgents, trying to trap them in their jungle bases and destroy them. Tree-jumping was one of several novel techniques they adopted: it involved parachuting into the jungle canopy from a height of only 500ft, allowing the parachute lines to catch in the trees, and then abseiling down a 250ft rope. From 1952 to 1957, the SAS accounted for over 100 of the insurgents killed or captured, and so proved their worth as an integral part of British counter-insurgency operations.

forces from firing on each other, the squadron commander made use of easily identifiable landmarks, such as rivers or ridge lines. In the early stages of the Emergency, teams jumped into the jungle, but as the landings in the trees were often dangerous and produced a crop of injuries, later patrols would walk to their objective or be inserted by helicopter. Each troop remained in direct contact with the squadron HQ and provided a SITREP (situation report) every night. As the troops radioed in, their reports were collated and then dispatched to the regimental HQ at Kuala Lumpur for further analysis.

The troops would usually operate within an area for up to 14 days – the maximum length of time between air-drops. As each man carried rations for two weeks, re-supply was vital after this length of time. However, the approach of an aircraft, its circling over the pre-arranged drop zone and the sight of several billowing parachute canopies would alert any bandits in the area and compromise the mission. Troops very rarely stayed in one area after receiving supplies, preferring to head immediately for a new operational base.

After a process of trial and error, the SAS troops settled into a routine that combined caution with aggression. The troop leader would establish a secure base camp from where three- or four-man patrols would be dispatched to cover the jungle within a four-mile radius. Camps were set up near a fresh-water supply with easily defended approaches. Trip flares and bamboo booby-traps were placed to cover the perimeter. The camp itself was never left empty; while two patrols were scouring the area, another group would remain behind to protect the troop's food and ammunition, and above all, their only means of communicating with the outside world, the radio.

In the eerie, twilight world of the Malayan jungle, patrols had to move with great caution, ever wary of sudden ambush, through some of the most unforgiving and treacherous terrain in the world. Cooper recalled that even nature seemed to conspire against the men:

Below left: Sergeant Paddy Hannah retrieves his parachute after a successful jump into the jungle.

Below: SAS men boarding an aircraft before the Belum Valley operation of 1952. Despite the danger of injury involved in parachuting through the jungle canopy, the ability to insert soldiers rapidly into the combat zone justified the risk. However, as helicopters became more widely available they superseded parachuting as a method of landing troops and tree-jumping was abandoned.

Right: An SAS trooper in Malaya in 1960. He wears jungle-green drill fatigues, and the badge of Malaya Command is worn on the upper sleeve. Most of his equipment is carried in the ubiquitous bergen knapsack. On his head is a bush hat and his boots are a combination of canvas and rubber. To cut through the thick jungle, he carries a machete. His armament is a 9mm Owen sub-machine gun. This unusual Australian weapon has its magazine mounted on the top of the receiver. The barrel can easily be changed, which simplifies maintenance.

Above: The pilot of a Valetta during a supply-dropping mission. Inset right: Crated supplies leave a Valetta destined for an SAS patrol in the jungle.
Far right: Drop Zone 'B', near a plantation in Malaya. SAS units operating deep in the jungle needed to be supplied regularly in order to function. Road supply was out of the question, and so RAF transport conducted re-supply by air.

'In secondary jungle, often areas of dense bamboo, w had to do a lot of cutting with our machetes and didn move very quickly. Worse, the noise we made carried fo miles if it wasn't masked by the screams of monkeys When we moved through swamps, the noise was terribl and, covered in leeches, we were lucky to cover 200yd i an hour.

'Moving through primary jungle was much easier a there was little ground vegetation, but we had to watc out for snakes. We tried to avoid well-used tracks as th CTs often set up ambushes or pig traps of sharpened bamboo along the way.'

The perseverance of the SAS teams in the endless round c patrolling did pay dividends on several occasions. In Augus 1956 Sergeant Turnbull and three troopers tracked four CT for five days until the enemy reached their base. Waiting until a rainstorm forced a sentry into the group's basha (hut) the patrol attacked and in a brief firefight neutralised th guerrillas. Towards the end of the Emergency, in Februar 1958, 37 men of D Squadron led by Major Thompson para chuted into the Telok Anson swamp in Selangor and after 1 weeks forced two bands of guerrillas to surrender.

Those men who remained pursued the enemy with dogged determination

Constant action placed great strains on the squadrons and many were well below strength through illness and injury but those men who remained continued to pursue the enem with dogged determination. One of the most spectacular and important successes was the ambush of Ar Poy, one of the CTs' district officials, by Muir Walker and some men from Squadron. On a routine patrol, the team found a well-buil basha and packed the bamboo supports with plastic explo sive. Signs of recent use suggested that a party of CTs wa: still in the area, so the patrol settled down to wait for the enemy. As Cooper recalled, it was to be two weeks before the ambush was sprung:

'There were three men in the ambush party at any one time. They were relieved every 24 hours and went back to a camp, 2200yd deeper in the jungle. We had a se routine: no smoking, no cooking, no talking, and a craw line running out for 300yd to the "toilet". Our body odour: were completely different from those of the CTs because of our different diets.

'After 14 days of watching, the enemy finally turned up Trooper O'Brien was on duty at the time, and when the four Chinese entered the basha he pushed the plunger - nothing happened. After so much rain, the explosive wa: useless. O'Brien was alone and couldn't signal back fo: fear of alerting the enemy. He waited until they came ou onto the balcony and then opened fire with his Belgian FN FAL rifle. He killed Ar Poy, who was the District Commit tee Secretary.'

The removal of a high-ranking official was a major blow to

Above: An elephant carrying supplies for the SAS. To help transport supplies in the Malayan jungle, it was decided to import a number of Thai elephants used in logging operations. The animals duly arrived and were loaded up for their first trip into the jungle. However, these elephants were not used to jungle, but to the forests of Thailand. They panicked at the sight of the unfamiliar terrain, sitting down and rolling over. The important cargo of rations was crushed. The elephants were sent home to resume their preferred duties and the SAS continued to rely on aerial supply drops.

both the organisation and prestige of the CT units working the area. Without leadership, short of food, and bombarde by propaganda from 'voice' aircraft and pamphlets urgir them to surrender, many left the jungle and gave themselve up to the authorities.

Faced by the growing success of the British counter insurgency effort, several of the leading figures in the C movement fled to the relative security of Thailand. Her untroubled by the ineffectual Thai Army, they were able direct the activities of bandit groups by radio. The milita. authorities were quick to recognise that the closure infiltration routes across the border and the destruction the enemy's transmitter would severely hamper their abili to wage a guerrilla campaign. The SAS squadrons were th ideal choice to carry out such operations.

On one occasion, an SAS radio picked up wireless tran missions; the station appeared to be located somewhe between Kota Bahru and Alor Star, possibly in the Valley No Return. B Squadron, led by Johnny Cooper, was given th task of finding and destroying the radio. Flown to Kota Bah by the RAF, the squadron then sailed down the Kelant river to Tanach Merah, the starting point for the mission.

During the slow, tortuous march to the valley, Coope became acutely aware that the squadron had a maximum 14 days to find the station:

'First, we had to go over the Anak Reng, a 6000ft ridge. took 12 days of hard slogging to reach the summit and b that time most men had lost a lot of weight. There was r sign of CT activity so I split the squadron into troops cover more ground. Our rations were running out an once we had taken an airdrop, our cover would hav been blown.

'On the 13th day, Bernard Mills and his troop wer working their way down a very narrow defile and hear the sound of gushing water. Mills went forward to carr out a recce and discovered a waterwheel. The CTs ha blocked the river channel and the waterwheel wa connected to three Bedford generators, producir enough power to run the wireless.

'Mills and his men got into position, went in ar clobbered everybody in the station. The destruction of vital link between the local CTs and their leaders Thailand helped to undermine bandit activity in th border region.'

In various guises, the SAS fought throughout the critical yea of the Malayan Emergency. The counter-insurgency w was always unglamorous and often unrewarding, yet the S/ squadrons found a niche in unconventional warfare that the alone were able to fill. In helping to defeat the CTs in Malay the SAS had also assured their own future; a future that wou take them to the scorching desert of Oman and the battle f the Jebel Akhdar.

2

ASSAULT ON THE JEBEL AKHDAR

The SAS in Oman

OMAN AT WAR

When D Squadron, 22 SAS, arrived in Oman in November 1958, the country had been in the throes of civil war for about 16 months. Rebels, determined to overthrow the autocratic regime of Sultan Said bin Taimur and to establish a theocratic state under the Imam of Oman, Ghalib bin Ali, were well-ensconced on the mountainous plateau of the Jebel Akhdar in the north of the country. In June 1958 Ghalib's brother, Talib, had landed in Oman with some 80 armed men and moved onto the Jebel. The Sultan reacted by deploying troops against the rebels, but Sheikh Suleiman bin Himyar, the powerful leader of the Beni Riyain Jebel tribe, who was already at odds with the Sultan over the right to grant oil-exploration licences, rose up in support of the Imam, and the Sultan's Armed Forces (SAF) were forced to withdraw. In desperation, the Sultan requested aid from Britain. The delicate situation in the Middle East ruled out the extensive employment of British armed forces in Oman and so, with the back-up of a detachment of Life Guards equipped with Ferret armoured cars, elements of the Trucial Oman Scouts, and RAF units based in Aden, a small SAS force was committed to flush out the rebels.

ON A HOT and humid day in mid-November 1958, several transport aircraft lumbered down the runway of an airfield in Malaya and took to the air on a northwesterly heading. On board were the 80 or so men of D Squadron, 22 SAS, a beefed-up squadron fully equipped and ready for operations, but with little idea of where they were going. As the aircraft left the Malayan peninsula behind, the men speculated on their final destination. The clue lay in the hectic days of preparations they had recently made. A corporal serving with the squadron remembered the training:

'Everything was done in the full heat of the day. We set up a series of hard marches with bergens [rucksacks] weapons and ammunition, and at the end of each march there was more and more range work. More and more open work, as opposed to work which we'd always done in jungle, and longer range marksmanship, well over the 25 or 30yd which we had previously engaged in.'

Throughout this period, the secret had been well-kept. Only the CO, Lieutenant-Colonel Tony Deane-Drummond, the ops officer and the squadron commander, Major Johnny Watts, were party to it, but the shrewder members of the squadron had a pretty good idea it was to be somewhere in the Middle East. As the aircraft pulled up on the airstrip on the island of Masirah and the squadron was finally briefed their suspicions were confirmed – they were in Oman and their target was the Jebel Akhdar.

The Jebel Akhdar (Green Mountain) rises precipitously from the Omani desert to form a sheer and formidable massif topped by a plateau and surrounded by jagged peaks rising to 10,000ft. For some time this mountain stronghold had been the domain of rebel forces opposed to the regime of Sultan Said bin Taimur. The rebels were well armed with

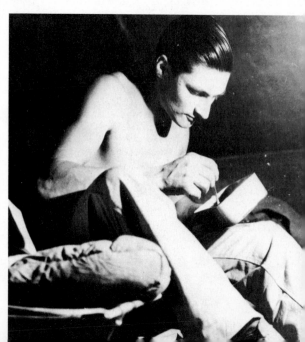

mortars, light machine guns and rifles and had dug themselves in with prepared fortifications and a system of deep caves for protection from aerial harassment. Although mainly contained within the confines of the Jebel, the rebels had successfully resisted any attempts by the Sultan's Armed Forces (SAF), assisted by detachments of British Life Guards, Trucial Oman Scouts and Aden-based RAF units, to take the Jebel. Frustrated by the stalemate, specialist help was requested and on 18 November the SAS arrived on mainland Oman.

'The sergeant medic got blown up on four separate occasions'

D Squadron quickly set out for the area of operations in a column of one-tonners under Captain Peter de la Billière, but soon ran into trouble. A member of the squadron recalls the perilous trek along the road to Nizwa which was strewn with rebel mines:

> 'That was a journey and a half. I myself was blown up twice in two different trucks. The mines they were using were both Soviet and American but luckily they were anti-vehicle mines, mainly concerned with knocking the vehicle off, so you tended to find yourself driving along at one moment and then sitting on your arse in the desert the next after a spectacular explosion and all sorts of bits of metal flying around. I remember there was one really unfortunate guy, Bill Evans, who was the sergeant medic, who got blown up on four separate occasions. Every truck he climbed onto got blown up. By the end he was thoroughly shell-shocked and a bit ga-ga.'

Battered and bruised, caked with dust and dirt, two of the squadron's troops arrived in Nizwa while the other two split off to the north side of the Jebel, to a place known as the Persian Steps. From the village of Tanuf on the south side and the Persian Steps on the north, D Squadron began operations on the Jebel.

It was tough acclimatising to their new conditions. Malaya had been hot, wet and humid but on the Jebel it was

Page 27: Captain Peter de la Billière and Major John Watts (foreground) on a reconnaissance mission on the Jebel Akhdar. Above: An aerial photograph of the Tanuf Slab, where the SAS launched a diversionary attack during the assault on the Jebel Akhdar. The SAS initiated aggressive patrols on the Jebel, regularly scaling the rugged mountainside at night. The information gained from these outings and from aerial reconnaissance was to put to use in planning the final assault. Far left: Sergeant medic Bill Evans with his 'magic spoon' in action. Evans, blown up four times on the Jebel, was well-known for his ability to eat faster than anyone else.

29

Above: Sergeant 'Herbie' Hawkins won a Distinguished Conduct Medal on the Jebel.
Below: A 0.3in Browning in support of de la Billière's cave raid.

scorching by day and bitterly cold at night. There was little vegetation and precious little water. They were also up against a very different enemy. One of the participants on the first OP patrol (24-hour reconnaissance) recounts his troop's first contact on the Tanuf Slab:

'We got to the top and we found positions that the enemy had obviously occupied, so we decided to get into their positions rather than make new ones of our own, because we knew enough about them to realise that they would spot a new position on the skyline the same as we would if it was our area. At about 0630 the sun came up and we fried and fried and fried. We had two extremes. At night it was cold enough on top of the mountain to freeze the water bottle, and we weren't as well equipped then as we are today. All we had were OG [olive-green] trousers and jacket and a very thin standard issue pullover. We didn't take sleeping-bags on a 24-hour recce since all they did was slow you down, and anyway, we didn't intend to sleep, not knowing whether they had established night picquets.

'Around about 1400 hours I had another three men with me in my patrol and we were looking down and covering an area when, lo and behold, I saw this Arab start making his way up. He got up to within about 300yd of us when he must have spotted some sort of movement because he shouted up at me, obviously thinking I was one of them. So we shouted down, but then he decided, having had his rifle on his shoulder in the sling position, that something wasn't quite right here, so he took it off whereupon I shot him. My mate alongside me shot him as well and we just blew him away. Within 30 seconds we were under fire from numerous places. They were hyperactive and their reaction was perfect and they started shooting from all

areas and concentrating on us. Further along the ridge, the other half of our troop was trapped and one of them, Corporal "Duke" Swindells, was shot.'

With the aid of RAF Venoms blasting the rebel positions with rockets, the troop managed to extract itself and thereafter the SAS confined its reconnaissance to night patrolling, out of the fiery heat of the day and with less chance of being spotted and overwhelmed by numerically superior rebel forces. The SAS men also developed a keen respect for their opponents, who were trained and highly professional.

'Three rounds rapid from the Carl Gustav went straight in the middle'

The patrolling continued as the squadron got the hang of the terrain and the rebel tactics and positions. On one patrol, carried out by de la Billière's troop, Arabs were observed disappearing into a large cave. In a war that so far had presented the SAS with little in the way of specific targets to hit, it was decided to follow up the recce with a strike on the hide out. A machine gunner who went up the Jebel that night remembers the action:

'As de la Billière's troop had done the recce, they would do the nearest bit and would put a 66mm rocket or Carl Gustav rocket into the cave – several in fact. Our troop was designed to cover them and we were on a slightly higher ridge about two or three hundred yards above them. We climbed up that night, early morning came and I was behind the Browning. I had persuaded Johnny Watts that the ideal weapon for Oman was the .30 Browning where you had the range you didn't have with the LMG, but, like all machine guns, it attracts a lot of attention. We set the gun up overlooking the cave and then, first thing in the morning, several men came to the entrance of the cave and were about to start leading the donkeys out. Whereupon, three rounds rapid from the Carl Gustav went straight in the middle and *Whoof*, they blew the cave in and a fair number of them to pieces. Once again, within a minute and a half, we were all under attack. They were amazing in their reactions plus their knowledge of the ground. They were born for it and their reactions were fast. We were under attack from their mortars. We were under attack from their LMGs and from individual tribesmen who were all spoiling for a fight. So, with the help of my machine gun and the RAF who arrived – we had them on a sort of taxi-cab system – we extracted ourselves without loss.'

But not everything was going D Squadron's way and there were several sticky moments that could have had disastrous consequences were it not for the men's superb fitness and cool-headedness when in a tight corner. One of the problems was the lack of good maps and detailed information on the inhospitable terrain on the heights of the Jebel. On one occasion, acting on information provided by a British officer seconded to the SAF, a half troop found itself on the

For the troops of D Squadron the conditions on the Jebel were entirely different from those they had left behind in the Malayan jungles. The rock of the Jebel is hard and metallic; silent movement is extremely difficult. Ordinary-issue nail-shod boots not only made a great deal of noise but soon came apart on the rough and abrasive surface. Deep-sided ravines slice their way through the plateau and, to cover even a short distance, SAS patrols had to spend many hours climbing and descending the sheer, rocky faces. Sounds, echoing through the ravines, played strange tricks on the troopers – a sudden noise from 300yd away could seem to come from behind a nearby rock. Living off the land was impossible, so the SAS patrols had to carry all rations and equipment with them. Since patrolling required the use of climbing ropes to negotiate particularly difficult terrain, the troopers were always well laden. Donkeys were used on occasion to transport their gear, but the small donkeys imported from Somalia proved useless on the alien Jebel terrain. To make matters worse, the climate on the Jebel alternated between sub-zero temperatures at night and scorching heat during the day.

Above: The village of Saiq, captured by the SAS on 30 January 1959. The hide-out of one of the rebel leaders, Suleiman, was nearby. 'Suleiman's cave' as it became known, yielded a treasure-trove of guerrilla weapons.

razor-edge Muti ridge on the eastern side of the Jebel shortly before sunrise. Their NCO recounts how they nearly got wiped out:

'We got to a certain point and above us, some 250ft away, was the summit. As always, we got ourselves into fighting positions and were about to send out a patrol. In the usual SAS manner we sat about for 10 minutes in absolute silence when, lo and behold, we heard these two Arabs talking to each other above us. There we were in a position where you couldn't go backwards, you couldn't go forwards and we were totally exposed. We couldn't get to them so we made ourselves comfortable and hoped against hope that we could spend the day there without them seeing us and then move on the next night. It got daylight and by that time we felt there were between six and ten up there. As the dawn light came they had a good look around and spotted the two SAF blokes who had come with us.... They thought we'll have these no bother at all.... they were sending exploratory shots pinging all over the place, and we wanted to draw their fire to see if we could knock off a couple. So I took an empty soup tin and said to the guy who was with me, "OK, put the can on the end of your rifle and poke it up and see if that'll draw their fire and I'll engage them." That didn't work, so then we put a cap comforter on the end of the rifle and poked it out. That drew an immediate response of shots but they weren't going to show themselves because they'd read the same cowboy books as we had. We then realised, through a lot of shouting and hoo-ha, that they were going to bring up reinforcements and have our scalps so we called Johnny Watts up and explained the situation. Everyone was roundly cursed.

'To deal with the situation, mortars were brought up

and the RAF called in. Whilst this mortaring was going on we decided that, come hell or high water, we had to extract, so, by a series of leapfrogs, we went past each other and got off the ridge and lower down. They pursued us all the way.'

By this time, the Life Guards' Ferret armoured cars had come up to spray the rebels with Browning machine-gun fire and, finally, the pursuing rebels were driven off, back into the haven of the Jebel. Miraculously, the SAS had escaped unscathed, the only casualty being one of the SAF Baluchis who had received a bullet in the backside for his pains. Everyone else had only a few cuts and bruises.

It was clear that the Jebel would have to be stormed in force

By Christmas, despite some SAS operational successes, the rebels were still firmly entrenched on the Jebel and the stalemate continued. It was clear that to gain control of the plateau, the SAS would require more manpower and that the Jebel would have to be stormed in force. To this end, A Squadron, under the command of Major Johnny Cooper, was brought in from Malaya to join D Squadron for the final push. Cooper's reinforcements flew out in four aircraft to Awabi on the northern side of the Jebel, and from there they motored down to the Persian Steps and climbed up to the positions held by Rory Walker's two troops from D Squadron.

Major Cooper's newly arrived squadron was soon in

Below: Captain Rory Walker and one of his men of D Squadron on the Jebel Akhdar near Suleiman's cave (encircled and arrowed in photograph).

action against rebel positions on a mountain whose twin peaks led to its being christened 'Sabrina'. Unlike D Squadron, they were not acclimatised to the wintry conditions and their CO remembers the hardships they encountered:

'It was the coldest winter for God knows how long. We had arctic sleeping-bags, cold and wet weather equipment – it was really freezing. We had a lot of parachute drops up there, especially of mortar bombs, and we had to use the parachutes to keep warm. There was rain, freezing sleet, snow – it was horrible. And we'd come straight from Malaya.'

In mid-January 1959, several attacks were launched on Sabrina and around Tanuf on the south side to tie down the main rebel forces. These, however, served a dual purpose, in that they were also part of a simple, yet cunning, deception that was crucial to the whole operation. The two squadrons of 22 SAS were massively outnumbered by the rebels, and the element of surprise had to be exploited to the full.

The key decision was where to attack. A full frontal assault into well-defended positions would be suicidal, so any of the known approach routes was out. In a twin-engined Pioneer,

Tony Deane-Drummond and his two squadron commanders, Johnny Watts and Johnny Cooper, reconnoitred the area, looking for a possible way up the Jebel to take its defenders unawares. After scouring the terrain they decided upon a strenuous but climbable route, not even a track, running from the village of Kamah up between the Wadi Kamah and the Wadi Suwaik. An on-the-ground recce by members of de la Billière's troop revealed the presence of a 0.5in Browning machine-gun post but no in-depth defence. This would be their point of entry.

To reinforce the deception, the Arab donkey handlers were told that the attack was to go in from Tanuf. They were instructed, on pain of death, to tell no one of the plan. Within nine hours the rebels on the mountain were preparing to take on the SAS in the heights above Tanuf.

Far left: Members of 22 SAS are briefed before the assault on the Jebel.

Far left below: An Arab donkey loaded with ammunition. Their handlers were given false information about the direction of the main attack. They duly passed this on to the rebels, and the assault achieved the important advantage of surprise.

Jebel Akhdar
22 SAS, January 1959

When D Squadron, 22 SAS, was first deployed in Oman in November 1958, the mountain stronghold of the Jebel Akhdar was held by well-armed and entrenched rebel forces. Early in January A Squadron arrived, and 22 SAS started preparations for a decisive assault on the Jebel. At 0300 on 26 January the first phase of the operation began with A Squadron's attack on the Aquabat al Dhafar.

Taking Sabrina

26 Jan 0300 A Sqn reaches 'Sabrina' from the north side of the Jebel and secures the rebel position after a fierce firefight. Leaving 4 Troop to hold the summit, A Sqn pushes on to Tanuf.
1800 A Sqn joins D Sqn in Tanuf. Leaving one troop behind to mount a diversionary attack, the two squadrons travel by lorry to Kamah.

The final assault

2030 A Sqn leads the advance up the ridge towards 'Vincent'. D Sqn takes the lead and pushes on to 'Pyramid'.
27 Jan 0500 'Pyramid' is secured and elements of D Sqn begin the final ascent to 'Beercan'.
0630 'Beercan' is secured: the Jebel is in the hands of 22 SAS and mopping up operations begin.

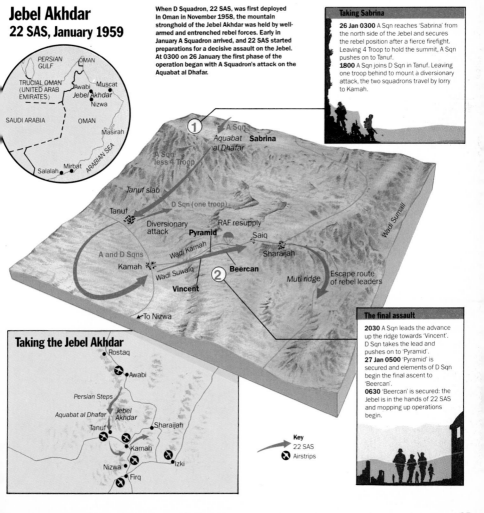

Taking the Jebel Akhdar

Key
22 SAS
Airstrips

With the whole of D Squadron in Tanuf, the first phase of the operation was launched by Cooper's A Squadron on Sabrina at 0300 hours. Cooper describes the assault:

'I attacked Aquabat al Dhafar with three troops while one, with all the machine guns from the others, laid a barrage on Sabrina. Tony Jeapes' troop was the one that scaled the pinnacle on the high side and got over the top and killed three or four. When Tony got on the top and scarpered these boys, he poured fire down on the other side and won the firefight. He had Corporal Wright shot up in the groin. Wright was the only casualty that Tony had, but Tony himself was very lucky. A chap had a misfire at point-blank range as Tony went over the top of a sangar [rock shelter]. By morning my three troops had Sabrina, and the enemy retreated.'

For his part in the action, Jeapes was awarded the Military Cross.

The attack on Sabrina held the enemy's attention and reinforcements were dispatched from the village of Saiq on the plateau to retake the position. Meanwhile, A Squadron left Sabrina and headed down to Tanuf to join D Squadron for the final push. The operation was going according to plan.

By 1800 hours on 26 January, A Squadron was in Tanuf catching a couple of hours' sleep. Both squadrons were then loaded into trucks and they set off by a roundabout route to the assembly area at Kamah, where they arrived after dark. At 2030, at the same time as a diversionary attack was mounted up the Wadi Tanuf by a troop left behind to further the deception, they crossed their start line.

The two squadrons, despite the favourable reconnaissance regarding enemy strength in the area, were heavily loaded with weapons and ammunition as they began the back-breaking slog up the Jebel. Johnny Cooper recalled

Above: One of the peaks of the Aquabat al Dhafar, nicknamed Sabrina. Here Tony Jeapes won a Military Cross by leading his troop in an aggressive assault on the mountain.

Below: Lieutenant-Colonel Deane-Drummond after the assault on the Jebel. The Bren guns in the foreground were captured from the rebels, along with a number of Lee-Enfields and 19th-century Martini-Henry rifles.

Right: A trooper of 22 SAS in Oman, 1959. He wears olive-green drill trousers, an airborne forces' 'Denison' smock and a woollen cap comforter. He carries a British 7.62mm L4A4, a revision of the Bren design to accommodate the standard Nato calibre round. At the waist he carries belt order based on the 1944-pattern belt plus water-bottle carriers.

Above: Several years after the assault on the Jebel Akhdar, Johnny Cooper returned for a visit. Here he is shown with an Omani tribesman.

the first moves as they worked their way up towards the thre objectives, code-named Vincent, Pyramid, and the fin summit, Beercan:

'We went up, my squadron (A) leading, and we got Vincent. John Watts' D Squadron went through me ar then, going along towards the ridgeline that went up Pyramid, we had to drop down. We lost about 1500 There was no time for reconnaissance and it was dark. was bloody difficult and we were carrying a hell of a lot weight.'

By 0500 the following morning D Squadron held Pyramid ar was poised to advance on Beercan. It was essential to secur the commanding position above at Beercan by daybreak, s Deane-Drummond and Johnny Watts decided to lighten th men's loads down to essential weapons and ammunition ar make a dash for the summit. An hour-and-a-half late exhausted from ten hours of solid climbing, two troops from held Beercan. The heavy Browning, discovered by de Billière's preliminary recce, was seized and the SAS took parachute resupply.

So successful was the ruse that the two squadrons encour tered minimal opposition. To many it seemed an anticlima but, as they consolidated their positions on the top of th Jebel, all were thankful that casualties had been so ligh Tragically though, a sniper's bullet had struck a grenade i one of the men's rucksacks, seriously wounding Trooper Carter, Bembridge and Hamer. Carter and Bembridge late died of their wounds.

In the wake of the SAS spearhead came the Life Guard and troops of the SAF. The SAS moved on into the rebe villages of Saiq and Sharaijah, where tribesmen were dis armed and caches of weapons and documents unearthec The rebel leaders, Suleiman, Ghalib and Talib, were nc where to be found. They had escaped down the Jebel an had disappeared into Saudi Arabia. Leaderless, the rebe surrendered easily, although none was happy about hand ing over his arms. A few isolated pockets of resistance wer dealt with over the next few days and by 5 February the Jebe was firmly in the hands of the SAS.

A number of 'show the flag' marches and firepowe demonstrations were then put on, and a 'hearts and mind programme was carried out by SAS medics; the tribesmen c the Jebel soon shrugged off their fear of the SAS and SAF an forgot their loyalty to their erstwhile leaders.

The Jebel operation was a classic example of SAS ir tervention, where a small force of highly skilled troops an imaginative planning, coupled with solid air support, ca achieve results far beyond the scale of a more conventiona military strategy. Major (now Lieutenant-Colonel) Johnr Cooper, is, however, more pragmatic in his appraisal:

'It had to be done quickly. If you'd sent in a battalion c infantry it would have cost a lot of money. Here you wer sending only a small gang. It was an SAS job because w had the ability to carry pack-mule loads and we were a very fit.'

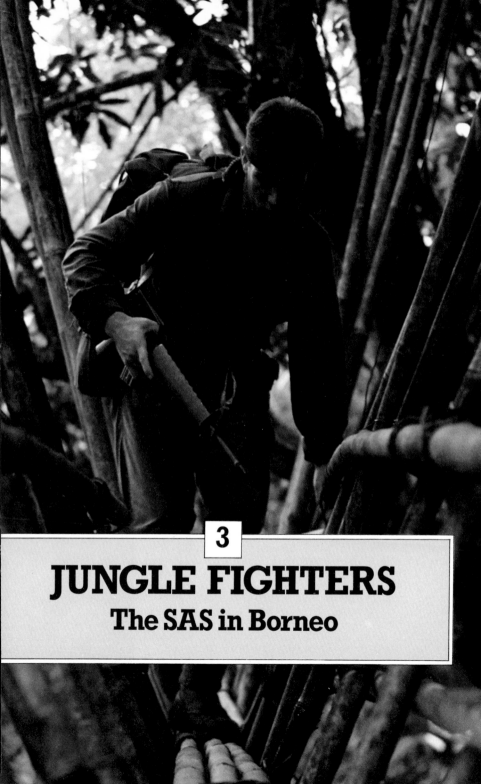

3

JUNGLE FIGHTERS
The SAS in Borneo

'I REGARD 70 troopers of the SAS as being as valuable to me as 700 infantry in the role of hearts and minds, border surveillance, early warning, stay behind, and eyes and ears with a sting!' So wrote Major-General Walter Walker, Commander British Forces, Borneo, in January 1964.

In the early hours of 28 April 1965 a four-man team of soldiers from the 22nd Special Air Service Regiment (22 SAS) waited patiently, SLRs at the ready, by the side of a river located some 9000yd inside Indonesian territory. The team, led by Captain Robin Letts, had been ordered to reconnoitre the area around Berjonkong and Achan, where the Indonesians were known to have forward bases. During his 'recce', Letts discovered a waterway used by the enemy to ferry men and supplies to the border, and decided to set up an ambush. Positioning his men inside the loop of the river, with one man to his right, one to his left, and the other covering the left flank, Letts awaited the arrival of Indonesian boats.

He did not have to wait long. At 0815, two-and-a-half hours after the team had taken up their positions, a boat appeared, followed by a second and then a third. Each boat contained three soldiers, two paddling and the other, holding a rifle, standing astern acting as sentry. As the first boat reached the man to Letts' right, the second Letts himself, and the third the man to Letts' left, the SAS team opened fire. It was all over within four minutes. Four Indonesian bodies lay floating in the water; two more lay dead in their boats, while two others lay prostrate on the river bank; the ninth enemy soldier had fled in panic into the adjacent swamp. The ambush had succeeded. Letts' team collected their bergens and 'scooted' back towards the safety of Malaysian territory, happy in the knowledge that they had made the enemy feel insecure even on his own home ground.

Only five battalions maintained security over 80,000 square miles

That the SAS had been given such a mission was no real surprise, since by that time 22 SAS had spent over two years on the jungle frontier which divided Indonesian Borneo (Kalimantan) from Malaysian Borneo. Indeed, almost as soon as the SAS arrived in Borneo, in January 1963, it had been deployed along the border to act as a defensive intelligence network. At the time, the British commander in Borneo, Major-General Walter Walker, faced the twin threat of an internal uprising from the Clandestine Communist Organisation (CCO), a subversive movement based mainly on Chinese settlers in Sarawak, and of external invasion from Kalimantan. Apart from a small number of local forces, Walker had only five battalions of men available to meet these threats, an insufficient force to maintain internal security over the 80,000 square miles of territory on his side of the border, and at the same time to guard against possible attack from the other side. In the event, Walker decided to hold back the bulk of his men as a reaction force, ready to respond to troubles from within or incursions from without.

Previous page: An SAS trooper moves cautiously across a bamboo bridge in Borneo.
Below: An SAS detachment launches a narrow riverboat loaded with weapons and equipment at the outset of a patrol. In the countless waterways of Borneo, craft such as these were invaluable as transport.

At the same time he decided to deploy the available SAS squadron (about 70 men) along the border to warn of any Indonesian incursions.

The SAS had been allotted a most difficult task. One squadron, totalling not even 100 men, was being asked to keep watch along a jungle frontier almost 1000 miles long, a frontier so wild and rugged that in some places it had not even been mapped. But then the SAS had extraordinary qualities. More so than any other regiment, the SAS possessed the ability to operate in inhospitable terrain for long periods of time, living off the land without regular re-supply; moreover, having taken part in the counter-insurgency campaign of the Malayan Emergency (1948–60), many SAS

The assault on the Jebel Akhdar had confirmed that the SAS would be invaluable in the sort of small-scale fighting that tends to be associated with the problems of decolonisation. In recognition of this fact, in addition to the Territorial regiment, 21 SAS, and its progeny, 22 SAS, a second Territorial regiment, 23 SAS, was formed in 1959. The SAS enjoyed several years of peace following the end of the Malayan Emergency in 1959, but in the early 1960s, two new campaigns began.

The first was in Borneo, where SAS men were committed from 1963 to guard the borders of the new Federation of Malaysia against Indonesian-backed infiltration. This was a role admirably suited to the SAS and was crowned with victory in 1966. The other campaign was less satisfactory. This was the involvement in Aden and the Federation of South Arabia, where British troops were attempting to stem the tide of radical Arab nationalism. Deployed in the wild hill areas of the Radfan and in the city of Aden itself, the SAS could do little in a losing situation, and withdrew along with the rest of the British Army in 1967. The SAS wings are shown above.

JUNGLE PATROLS

The central part of the British military effort during the Borneo campaign was the insertion of SAS patrols into the jungle for weeks at a time, to gather intelligence on the strength, location and intentions of hostile forces.

The deployment of a handful of men under such conditions was a controversial subject during this period. Many countries held the view that small teams were very vulnerable to enemy action. The British, however, took the view that small groups of highly motivated men were ideal for use in this role and could achieve results out of all proportion to their size.

In Borneo, the four-man team was established as the basic tactical unit for these operations. Each patrol had three main areas of responsibility: monitoring the infiltration of guerrillas into friendly territory, gathering intelligence from the native population, and carrying out a 'hearts and minds' programme to win the friendship of the natives.

The value of SAS patrols depended on the ability of a few well-trained men, all specialists in a particular field, working as a mutually supportive and independent team.

On active duty, the standard SAS patrol always included a signaller and a medic, and the other two members might be a linguist, explosives expert or some other specialist. Each man had to carry all the supplies essential to an operation beyond the reach of the usual support services.

Movement through the jungle followed a set pattern: the patrol would be led by a scout, with the commander, medic and signaller following his path at spaced intervals. The last man usually carried a 7.62mm GPMG or Bren, the rest SLRs and M16s.

troopers spoke or understood Malay, the *lingua franca* of the frontier tribes. These attributes proved to be invaluable because in practice the only effective means of controlling the border was to enlist the support of the border tribes, the native people who lived in settlements located on hillsides or in river valleys.

Fortunately for the SAS, many of these tribes were well disposed towards the British. Nevertheless, the tribesmen loyalty could not be taken for granted, particularly as the favourite sport of some of them was headhunting. In an effor

THE SAS IN BORNEO

Between December 1963 and August 1966 the mountainous island of Borneo, sparsely populated and covered by dense jungle, became the scene of armed warfare. The former British colony of Malaya, west of Borneo, was pressing for the formation of a major new political entity in the area. To be known as the Federation of Malaysia, it was to comprise British North Borneo (now Sabah), Sarawak, Brunei, Malaya and Singapore. Though Britain endorsed the future that Malaya proposed for her territories, President Ahmed Sukarno of neighbouring Indonesia bitterly opposed the plan as a threat to his ambition to expand the Indonesian frontiers.

In December 1962 a rebellion led by anti-Malaysian elements erupted in the Sultanate of Brunei, though British forces arrived and suppressed the revolt before Sukarno could profit from it. Four months later, however, Sukarno began to infiltrate insurgents from Kalimantan (the Indonesian southern part of Borneo) into the British colonies. When Sabah and Sarawak (though not Brunei or Singapore) became officially incorporated into Malaysia in September 1963, the infiltrations were stepped up. In response, the British organised a border guard of Malaysian, British and Commonwealth troops to contain the insurgents. A prominent constituent of this force was the SAS.

So effective was the Allied force that the Indonesian incursions seldom penetrated much beyond the actual line of the border. As time passed, the cost of 'Confrontation' came to be considered too high, and the Indonesians lost faith in their president. Sukarno was overthrown in March 1966 and five months later Indonesia made peace with Malaysia.

Far left above: An SAS trooper scans the jungle vegetation for signs of the enemy.
Far left below: A patrol cooks up rations on a solid fuel stove deep in the jungle. The SAS was unable to rely on aerial resupply as it had during the Malayan Emergency, and in Borneo each man had to carry everything he needed for a patrol. Canned sardines, which were easily portable and did not require cooking, were an important constituent of the diet of the SAS.
Below: A patrol greets a native tribesman on the opposite bank of the river. The SAS used chance encounters with the indigenous peoples to win allies. They worked at a friendly, personal level, rather than relying on bureaucratic plans and policies imposed by higher authorities.

During the Confrontation with Borneo the SAS once again had the opportunity to employ its expertise in deep-penetration patrolling and raiding.
Right: Members of an SAS patrol moving through the jungles of Borneo.
Far right: An SAS signalman at a forward operating base.
Below right: An SAS trooper, in ambush position, scans the river for signs of enemy activity.

to win them over, SAS personnel operating in small teams of three to four men went into the settlements and stayed there for weeks or even months, helping with the planting, harvesting and weeding of crops, giving medical assistance and at all times respecting the customs and traditions of the natives. In return, the natives provided the SAS teams with news of any useful findings, such as spoors or bootmarks left in the jungle by the Indonesians.

Such information was relayed back to squadron headquarters on high-frequency radios and was supplemented by other information – about border-crossing points, jungle tracks, potential sites for ambushes and helicopter landings, and so on – gathered by the SAS teams on the patrols they carried out in their respective areas. So successful were these activities that by the time the Indonesians began their cross-border incursions, in April 1963, the SAS had already won over many of the tribes and had provided the security forces with 'eyes and ears' along the frontier.

SAS teams led ambush parties or 'killer groups' over the border

In the months that followed, the SAS continued their frontier duties, winning 'hearts and minds', collecting intelligence and detecting and tracking enemy incursions, as well as helping to train a force of native irregulars called the Border Scouts. Inevitably, though, as the Indonesians stepped up their guerrilla incursions, the regiment's role was modified. By early 1964 SAS personnel were not only detecting incursions but were also helping infantrymen to intercept the infiltrators; the infantry, deployed from forward bases or dropped into the jungle by helicopter, were guided into ambush positions by SAS teams. Later that year SAS teams led ambush parties or 'killer groups' over the border into Kalimantan, to hit the enemy before he could penetrate Malaysian territory.

These offensive forays, ultra-secret operations codenamed 'Claret', called for the utmost skill and care. Any trace of British presence on Indonesian soil could have caused severe embarrassment to the British government. After all, Britain was not at war with Indonesia and wanted to avoid any accusation that she was escalating the conflict (it was for this reason, and also because of the risk of killing friendly tribesmen, that air strikes into Kalimantan were ruled out). Claret missions were, therefore, subject to definite limitations. They were to be undertaken only by experienced jungle troops and were to be guided by the SAS and the Border Scouts, who were to reconnoitre the target areas beforehand. They were also limited in terms of depth of penetration – initially to 3000yd.

By the end of 1964, Claret operations had proved to be politically acceptable and militarily feasible. Consequently, when Walker learnt of a divisional strength build-up of high quality Indonesian troops opposite the First Division (the western part of Sarawak) in December 1964, he sanctioned

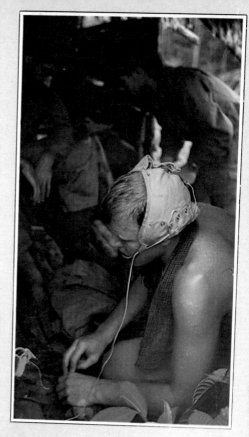

Jungle Fighters

Right: This Corporal of 22 SAS serving in Borneo in 1965 wears typical tropical kit: olive-green trousers, shirt of unidentified origin and battered jungle hat worn over a cloth-scarf sweat band. On his back he has a bamboo carrier, capable of lifting a wide variety of loads. A 1958-pattern web belt is worn around the waist, upon which is fixed – from left to right – an AR-15 ammunition pouch, 1944-pattern compass pouch, AR-15 ammunition pouch and 1944-pattern water-bottle carrier. Armament comprises the US-manufactured AR-15 Armalite assault rifle, fitted here with twin magazines. A highly effective weapon for close-quarters jungle fighting, the AR-15 proved popular with specialist troops such as the SAS and the Gurkhas. Unlike the regular forces, specialists such as the SAS can choose their weapons and equipment from among the best available; as a result, they often have an exotic range of kit.

Claret missions to a depth of 10,000yd. The Indonesians seemed to be planning a major offensive against the First Division, and Walker believed that by threatening their forward bases and lines of communication he would force them to concentrate on defensive rather than offensive plans. In effect, Walker saw Claret operations as a means of denying the Indonesians the military initiative.

At first, during December 1964 and the early months of 1965, Claret teams were ordered to concentrate primarily on reconnaissance, a natural prerequisite to strikes in that the Kalimantan side of the border with the First Division had not previously been investigated to any great extent. Accordingly, SAS went over the border to identify Indonesian bases, infiltration routes (actual and potential) and lines of communication, by land and water.

Perhaps typical of such operations was a four-man patrol that set out early in January 1965 to recce the area south of Gunong Brunei, where the Koemba river ran close to the border. This patrol, led by Trooper Bennett, had to negotiate steep hills, thick jungle, rocky streams and a 300yd wide swamp before reaching the river. All the same their endeavours were worth while. They brought back valuable information about the area and also managed to earmark ambush positions – particularly promising in the latter respect was a high rock from which movements along the river, and along an established track linking Seluas and Siding, could be watched.

Above: An SAS patrol breaks camp during a reconnaissance mission. When moving out, it was important not to leave anything behind that might give the enemy clues as to the patrol's size or intentions.

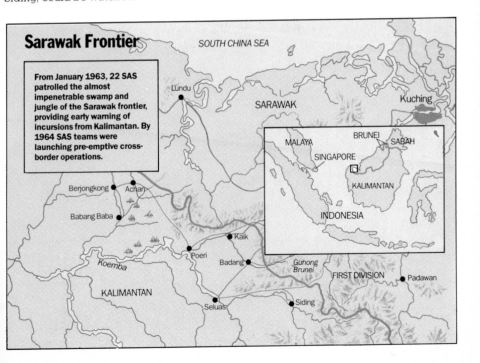

Sarawak Frontier

From January 1963, 22 SAS patrolled the almost impenetrable swamp and jungle of the Sarawak frontier, providing early warning of incursions from Kalimantan. By 1964 SAS teams were launching pre-emptive cross-border operations.

SOUTH CHINA SEA

Lundu

SARAWAK

Kuching

MALAYA

BRUNEI

SABAH

SINGAPORE

KALIMANTAN

INDONESIA

Berjongkong

Achan

Babang Baba

Kaik

Poeri

Badang

Koemba

Gunong Brunei

FIRST DIVISION

Padawan

KALIMANTAN

Seluas

Siding

If Letts' team had carried out a recce that ended up as an engagement, it was not long before such engagements became standard practice. By early May 1965, Major-General George Lea, who had succeeded Major-General Walker two months previously, had decided that Claret operations should begin in earnest. One of the objectives chosen was a major supply route, the Koemba river near Poeri. A four-man team of SAS troopers led by Don Large was ordered to investigate river traffic near Poeri and to engage a suitable target.

On their second day in the jungle the team heard enemy soldiers ahead

Large's team had taken on a well-nigh impossible mission. Six previous attempts had been made to reach this sector of the Koemba river – and each had been foiled by heavy going across swamps. The general feeling in headquarters was that this new attempt would also fail, but Large himself remained optimistic, even though soon after setting out from a landing position, on 10 May 1965, the patrol ran into difficulties. On their second day in the jungle the team heard

Main picture: A fortified SAS hill outpost with a large helicopter pad for bringing in supplies and launching heliborne operations. Helicopters were very important to the success of the campaign in Borneo, for they enabled wounded to be evacuated quickly and patrols to be inserted at short notice.
Right: A patrol leader examines a map to ascertain his position. In the jungle it was important not to rely on maps alone, as landmarks were often a better guide.

enemy soldiers ahead; they had to take a detour through thick undergrowth, and to do so without making a noise or leaving tracks, an endeavour that tested their jungle skills to the limit.

Worse was to follow. After crossing undetected over a main jungle track on the third day, and another main track (possibly used by the Indonesians for cutting off Claret teams) on the fourth day, the team made for a loop in the river, where Large believed they would find the tail of a spur leading to the river bank. To their chagrin all they found was more swamp – and each probe they made seemed to lead them into deeper swamp. After spending the night on a mud island, the team pressed on westwards, hoping to find higher ground. As they inched their way forward they heard the sound of boat engines – heavy diesels – but saw no sign at all of the spur. Failure began to seem inevitable, but Large refused to admit defeat. Taking breakfast on dry land, the team talked over their predicament and decided to persevere – to go back into the swamp and to head downstream with a view to finding a causeway to the river.

Progress was painfully slow, though they were at least encouraged by the sound of diesel engines, which indicated

Above: One of the ground rules for SAS operations in Borneo was the maintenance of good relations with the local people. Here a trooper practises minor surgery on a villager, cleaning out a gash prior to stitching. By gaining the trust and support of the people in the villages, the SAS were able to reap useful rewards.
Far right: Two local tribesmen acting as guide and pilot for an SAS river patrol.

that they must be close to the river. And then, to their surprise and amazement, they found high land rising to 30ft. It was the spur! They emerged from the swamp and began to negotiate the spur, soon entering a narrow belt of jungle. After crossing the jungle, they came to a rubber plantation. Skirting round this they saw before them the Koemba river, fast-flowing and some 40yd wide.

It was the sort of place the enemy would least expect an ambush

Having at last found his objective, Large wasted no time and proceeded to establish an observation post. He discounted the area to his right because there was little cover near the bank, and also rejected the area to his left, which, although well covered, was the first place the enemy would expect them to go. He settled for the area to his front, a 10ft-high river bank with a ditch on the near side. This position had its disadvantages, the greatest of which was that the team would have to pull back across open ground on their way out. But it afforded a good view of the river, a ditch in which to rest, and reasonable cover (in the form of scrub and a tree) for both bank and ditch. It was also the sort of place the enemy would least expect an ambush site, or so Large hoped.

During the afternoon Large observed movements on the river and planned his ambush. He came to the conclusion that the best means of fulfilling his strategic objective – to make the enemy feel that their major supply lines were threatened – would be to destroy a boat carrying war cargo. As regards tactics, he decided that his best bet would be to wait until a boat had negotiated the river bend and then open fire from astern; this would offer a good chance of causing serious damage and would limit the crew's opportunity to return fire. His plan of action was for his team members – Walsh, Millikin and Scholey – to move forward to firing positions, 3yd apart; he himself would move in behind them to direct the firing, to watch out for other boats and to keep an eye on the rear.

Having established their positions and plan of action for the ambush, Large and his team settled down to an unpalatable meal of uncooked meat-blocks – they were unable to use their solid-fuel stoves or light a fire for fear of giving themselves away – and then managed to catch some sleep. They were to spend the next day fulfilling the first part of their

During the early stages of the Borneo campaign the Indonesian-backed guerrillas held all the trump cards: they had intimate knowledge of the jungle and its dangers, knew how to live off the land, and used the local tribesmen as informants and providers of food. The small SAS patrols could not offset these advantages by military action alone, and adopted a 'softly-softly' approach to the problem.

The linchpin of their strategy was the 'hearts and minds' programme: a system of mutually beneficial exchanges between the local people and SAS teams. The way to success was gaining the confidence and trust of local tribesmen and the key figure was the patrol's medic who had to be prepared to deal with everything from gunshot wounds to births. Although the precise nature of a particular operation might vary, patrols followed a similar pattern of methods. They would enter the village unannounced and then seek out the headman. While some of the men engaged him in conversation, the medic would set up his surgery. Later, small presents would be exchanged and any urgent needs signalled back to base. The tribesmen would also be paid for any work they undertook for the SAS team. After a meal and more talk, the patrol would withdraw. Within the week, however, the SAS would reappear to take the next steps on the road to friendship.

SAS aid was not, however, purely altruistic; it produced military benefits. Villages were a valuable source of food, security and intelligence. If the locals could provide these facilities, the SAS would be free to concentrate on the destruction of the guerrilla forces operating in the jungle.

51

Above: An SAS patrol boards a truck on the edge of the jungle. Apart from the riverboat patrols, foot-slogging was the SAS's only means of transport in Borneo's tropical forests.

orders – to establish the pattern of river traffic. It soon became apparent that headquarters was fully justified in its assumptions about the importance of the river. Among the vessels the team saw go past were a military supply launch and a luxury motor cruiser. The latter was a tempting target, but it appeared to be the flagship of some VIP. Large was mindful of the political consequences that might result from the destruction of such a vessel and so let it alone. He also let pass a 40ft launch that carried soldiers, confident that a more suitable target would appear the next day – something it would be well worth while waiting for.

The next morning, having radioed for permission 'to engage opportunity target', Large and his colleagues waited eagerly. He allowed free passage to a two-man canoe and to a 30ft launch in the hope that a bigger prize might present itself. Five hours later none had done so, and as the sun became obscured behind thick cloud and rain began to pour down, Large's team-mates began to curse their leader's decision to let so many boats past on the previous day. But just then, with visibility fading, another launch appeared. It was a big one too, about 40ft long and 8ft wide; there were two sentries astern, it appeared to be carrying cargo, and soldiers were resting beneath its large canopy. As the launch passed by, 45yd distant, Large beckoned his men to their firing positions. Within half a minute they unleashed 60 rounds against their target, killing the two sentries and holing the boat. The stricken vessel listed in the water. As smoke belched from it, soldiers emerged from beneath the tarpaulin and jumped overboard as fast as they could. It was their only option, for, seconds later, the whole vessel was engulfed by flames.

Mission accomplished, the SAS men collected their effects together and took off along the spur as quickly as possible. However, there was a shock in store for them as Large found his path blocked, at head level, by a deadly snake – a king cobra – but fortunately the snake decided not to attack, and the team made rapid progress. By evening they had crossed the cut-off path. On the following day, having signalled for a helicopter on the SARBE (search and rescue beacon), they were winched out of the jungle and flown back to base. Large's sortie had accomplished a great deal. The team may only have destroyed one launch, but the psychological effect was devastating. The Indonesians now felt that their main supply routes were insecure and were compelled to re-deploy troops to guard them.

Other cross-border raids took place during the succeeding months, forcing the enemy further onto the defensive. In these subsequent raids, the role of the SAS was to act as guides, rather than sole participants, but that hardly mattered. The SAS men had done their bit. They had pioneered a tactic that was to force the Indonesians to abandon their forward bases and, in truth, to deny them any real chance of success.

4

THE SUPREME TEST
The Battle of Mirbat

AT 0530 HOURS, 19 July 1972, Captain Mike Kealy, a young officer commanding an eight-man SAS detachment in the small, remote town of Mirbat in Dhofar was awoken by the sound of shell-fire. He struggled to grab his equipment and rifle, while the room shook under the impact of further explosions close by, then hauled himself onto the roof of the fortified building that was his team's headquarters. In the cold light of dawn, with low cloud and a steady drizzle further hampering visibility, he tried to make out what was happening around him, little realising that he was about to take part in an action that would demonstrate beyond all doubt the fighting ability of the SAS; for without the courage, weapons skill and tactical acumen of all the SAS men involved, the town of Mirbat would surely have fallen to the vastly more numerous enemy.

As always in their operations, the SAS in Dhofar were keeping as low a profile as possible, using their expertise to support a government allied to Britain. The Sultanate of Oman, of which Dhofar was the isolated southern province, had a long history of association with the British – indeed, in

Page 53: A member of the SAS in Dhofar, armed with an L42A1 sniper's rifle and an M79 grenade launcher slung on his back.
Below: A patrol from one of the *firqat* units made up of former anti-government guerrillas and commanded by SAS men. Prior to 1970 the Dhofaris were alienated by the rule of Sultan Said bin Taimur, who exercised personal rule over Dhofar and imposed unpopular taxes. Said's son, Qaboos, overthrew his father in 1970 and instituted measures to gain the allegiance of the Dhofaris.

959 SAS troopers had spearheaded a decisive assault on
ie mountain fastness of rebels within Oman itself. The
ultan's domains were of great strategic importance in that
ieir northern tip, the Masandam peninsula, dominates the
iouth of the oil-rich Gulf. In 1969, in fact, some SAS men had
een deployed when it was suspected that a few Iraqi-
ained guerrillas might be operating there.

The people living in the mountainous hinterland of Dhofar
vere quite distinct both in their language and culture from
ie other subjects of the sultanate. Said bin Taimur, sultan
om 1932 to 1970, was a very conservative ruler. Every
spect of modern life – from radios to spectacles, from
iedicines to bicycles – was banned. Some Dhofaris, howev-
r, had found work abroad, and inevitably realised that the
nforced backwardness of their homeland was largely due
> the reactionary sultan. Swayed by the ideals of Arab
ationalism, a group of exiles formed the Dhofar Liberation
ront in 1962. In 1965 they started a small-scale guerrilla war
i Dhofar.

The Sultan's Armed Forces (SAF), comprising the Muscat
nd Northern Frontier Regiments, were able to contain the
isurgency at this stage, deploying about 1000 men in
•hofar, with British officers and Baluchis from Pakistan in the
inks.

Prisoners were publicly executed, and their bodies hung up for days

i 1967, however, the Marxist state of South Yemen (the
eople's Democratic Republic of Yemen) began to aid the
•hofari insurgents, who were, in any case, similar to the
emenis in language and culture. The Dhofari insurgents
ow had a safe base, and began to receive a flow of weapons
om the communist bloc; they were also given better
aining. The mountainous hinterland (known as the Jebel),
i which deep wadis, limestone caves and the lack of
ffective roads gave guerrillas natural advantages, was soon
ut of the control of the SAF, which had to content itself with
anging onto areas of the coastal plain.

Sultan Said's response to the revitalised insurgency was to
edouble stern repressive measures. Prisoners were pub-
cly executed and their bodies hung up for days, while
illages suspected of sympathising with the rebels were
ttacked, and their wells concreted over. The latter in
articular was a vindictive measure in a land where water is
t a premium.

Things went from bad to worse. The town of Rakyut,
dministrative centre of western Dhofar, fell to the adoo (as
ie guerrillas were known) on 23 August 1969. The capital of
•hofar, Salalah, was little more than a fortified enclave,
ontaining the town, the sultan's palace and an RAF base. A
vell-armed foe was steadily undermining an ally of Britain;
•ut it seemed little could be done.

In the spring of 1970, some senior SAS officers considered
ie problem of insurgency in Dhofar. The SAS had made

The campaign in Oman 1970–76
was the most important SAS
campaign between the end of the
Borneo Confrontation in 1966 and
the outbreak of the Falklands War.
In it the Regiment demonstrated its
ability to wage a long and patient
counter-insurgency campaign and
bring it to a successful conclusion.
The key to victory was to turn the
guerrillas' weapon of subversion
against them. The SAS
concentrated on winning back, by
providing medical and veterinary
care, those Dhofaris who
sympathised with the enemy.
They also conducted a public
relations campaign on behalf of the
Sultan, to convince the Dhofaris
that his modernisation programme
was a serious effort to improve
their lot. The Dhofaris were
encouraged to join the firqat,
irregular units of ex-guerrillas,
trained and led by SAS men. The
firqat although not always reliable
in combat, were useful for
gathering intelligence for the
regular government forces, the
SAF. In Oman, as in Borneo, the
SAS recipe of social service
combined with the personal touch
succeeded where coercion had
failed. The cap badge of 22 SAS is
shown above.

The Supreme Test

great use of good relations with local populations during th campaigns in Malaya and Borneo, and the senior officer concluded that a concerted attempt to win the 'hearts an minds' of the Dhofaris by establishing medical and veterin ary centres, coupled with a concentration on collecting th good intelligence that is the key to counter-insurgency, wa the essential first step in reversing the tide.

It was evident that under the rule of Sultan Said, such programme was impossible, but in July 1970 a palace cou (during which the old sultan shot himself in the foot) remove Said's control from the affairs of state. His son Qaboo Sandhurst trained and with experience in the British Arm enthusiastically set about implementing a new policy. H expanded his armed forces to include more fast patrol boat more helicopters and 12 Strikemaster jets; the SAF gre from 2500 to 12,000 men, led by some 600 British officers and few specialist NCOs, some on loan from the British Army an some under contract to the sultan. A whole series of mea sures was put into operation to improve the lot of the Dhofar and, crucially, an amnesty was offered to any of the *adoo* wh changed sides.

The first SAS team arrived in Dhofar within hours of th coup. One of their tasks was to act as a bodyguard for the ne ruler, but they also took a leading role in the implementatio of the new strategy. The SAS detachments were official named 'British Army Training Teams' (BATTs) so that it coul be denied that any British combat troops were present. Th first two training teams were based at Taqa and a small tow some 40 miles east of Salalah: Mirbat.

About 200 *adoo* surrendered between September 1970 and March 1971 alone – mainly due to disagreements between Marxists and more traditionalist Moslems. Qaboos was persuaded that these individuals could be used in a counter-insurgency role; and the SAS teams were to play a major part in this process.

The guerrillas who had surrendered were deployed in *irqat,* units of indeterminate size. Their loyalty was often in doubt, and the motives of many were questionable. Nevertheless, they formed an essential link with the local population, a link critical in the new strategy. In March 1971, the *irqat* showed that they could fight when a force of 60, together with 40 members of the SAS, penetrated the mountainous hinterland, and stayed for 12 days of almost constant fighting.

The broad sweep of government strategy was to show they could maintain control of eastern Dhofar while gradually establishing a presence in the mountains. Once the east was secure, and the guerrillas were no longer safe in their mountain strongholds, then a general move west could begin. To initiate this policy, two SAS squadrons led an offensive (Operation Jaguar) in October 1971, by *firqat* and SAF units, setting up a base inland, near Jibjat. This was complemented by Operation Leopard in the western Jebel, and Operation Simba on the border with South Yemen.

The decision of the guerrillas to attack Mirbat was their response to the fact that government forces were gaining the initiative. What better way to demonstrate the foolishness of changing sides and the continuing power of the *adoo* than by taking over a town in the east of Dhofar, and holding it for a few hours before substantial SAF troops could be moved in: a town moreover in which a British Army team had trained the local *firqat*?

The *adoo*, the guerrillas who fought against the sultan's forces, were a brave and resourceful foe whose possession of automatic weapons, especially the Russian Kalashnikov assault rifle, gave them formidable firepower. The original Dhofar Liberation Front was a broad grouping with radical Arab nationalist ideals. When, however, South Yemen became the main supplier of arms and protection, a Marxist ideology was adopted and the Liberation Front was subsumed into the People's Front for the Liberation of the Occupied Arabian Gulf (PFLOAG).

Most Dhofaris were not interested in Marxism as such. They were concerned about material progress (in particular the lack of it under Sultan Said), and yet fiercely tribal, especially in the mountains, and firmly Moslem. This gave Sultan Qaboos' modernisation programme and the tribally organised *firqat* a great attraction for many of the *adoo* offended by the extremes of PFLOAG ideology. Nevertheless, at the peak of the insurgency there were probably 200 full-time guerrillas ready for action, backed up by a 3000-strong militia.

As dawn began to break, the first elements moved forward

The attack on Mirbat was well planned. It was to take place during the monsoon period, when low cloud made air support difficult if not impossible (the town of Rakyut had fallen during the monsoon period when no air support had been available). A force of 250 guerrillas (far more than had ever been used in one operation before) had been assembled, and their support weapons included not only mortars and heavy machine guns, but also 75mm recoilless rifles, and one Carl Gustav 84mm rocket launcher. In order to weaken the *firqat* at Mirbat, a small group of *adoo* had allowed themselves to be observed near the foot of the mountain escarpment, and so a large proportion of the 60-strong *firqat* had been sent out to investigate. Finally, the attackers had reckoned the advantage of surprise as they stealthily surrounded the town and the fortified perimeter to its north during the night of 18/19 July 1972. They were undisturbed as they made for their start lines, and, as dawn began to break, the first elements began to move forward.

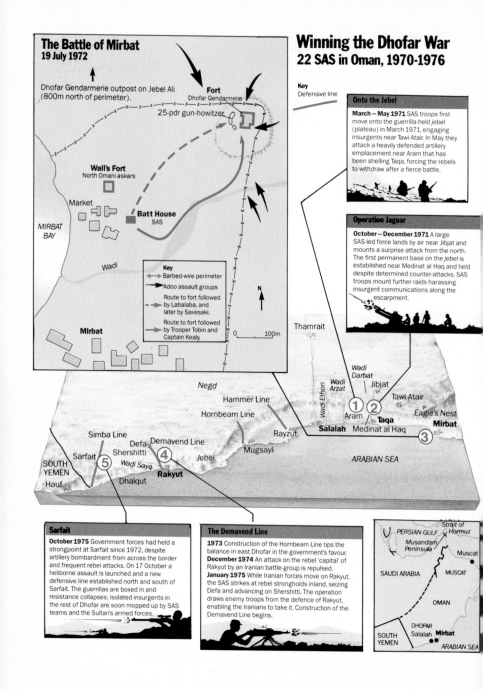

The Battle of Mirbat
19 July 1972

Dhofar Gendarmerie outpost on Jebel Ali (800m north of perimeter).

Fort
Dhofar Gendarmerie

25-pdr gun-howitzer

Wall's Fort
North Omani *askars*

Market

MIRBAT BAY

Batt House
SAS

Wadi

Mirbat

Key
- —x— Barbed-wire perimeter
- ➤ Adoo assault groups
- --➤ Route to fort followed by Labalaba, and later by Savesaki.
- ➤ Route to fort followed by Trooper Tobin and Captain Kealy.

N

0   100m

Winning the Dhofar War
22 SAS in Oman, 1970-1976

Key
Defensive line

Onto the Jebel

March – May 1971 SAS troops first move onto the guerrilla-held *jebel* (plateau) in March 1971, engaging insurgents near Tawi Atair. In May they attack a heavily defended artillery emplacement near Aram that has been shelling Taqa, forcing the rebels to withdraw after a fierce battle.

Operation Jaguar

October – December 1971 A large SAS-led force lands by air near Jibjat and mounts a surprise attack from the north. The first permanent base on the *jebel* is established near Medinat al Haq and held despite determined counter-attacks. SAS troops mount further raids harassing insurgent communications along the escarpment.

Thamrait

Negd

Hammer Line

Hornbeam Line

Rayzut

Wadi Darbat

Wadi Arzat

Jibjat

Tawi Atair

Eagle's Nest

Aram

Taqa

Mirbat

Salalah Medinat al Haq

① ② ③

Wadi Ethon

Simba Line

Defa

Sarfait

Shershitti

Demavend Line

Jebel

Mugsayl

SOUTH YEMEN

Wadi Saya

Rakyut

④

⑤

Dhalqut

Hauf

ARABIAN SEA

Sarfait

October 1975 Government forces had held a strongpoint at Sarfait since 1972, despite artillery bombardment from across the border and frequent rebel attacks. On 17 October a heliborne assault is launched and a new defensive line established north and south of Sarfait. The guerrillas are boxed in and resistance collapses; isolated insurgents in the rest of Dhofar are soon mopped up by SAS teams and the Sultan's armed forces.

The Demavend Line

1973 Construction of the Hornbeam Line tips the balance in east Dhofar in the government's favour.
December 1974 An attack on the rebel 'capital' of Rakyut by an Iranian battle-group is repulsed.
January 1975 While Iranian forces move on Rakyut, the SAS strikes at rebel strongholds inland, seizing Defa and advancing on Shershitti. The operation draws enemy troops from the defence of Rakyut, enabling the Iranians to take it. Construction of the Demavend Line begins.

Strait of Hormuz

PERSIAN GULF

Musandam Peninsula

Muscat

SAUDI ARABIA

MUSCAT

OMAN

DHOFAR

SOUTH YEMEN

Salalah **Mirbat**

ARABIAN SEA

Had total surprise been achieved, the attackers might well have won an easy victory. As it was, however, there was n outpost on a hill known as Jebel Ali, 800yd north of the barbed-wire perimeter. This was manned by a patrol of the Dhofar Gendarmerie, and fortunately for the defenders at Mirbat, this patrol noticed the *adoo* creeping up and opened fire. Four of the gendarmes were killed and four managed to escape, but their alertness meant that firing had begun rather earlier than the insurgent leaders had hoped. The support weapons opened up, wakening the SAS detachment. Kealy himself rushed to the roof of the 'Batthouse', as the BATT headquarters was called.

Kealy had only recently joined the SAS as a troop commander. At 23 years old he was rather less experienced than the eight men from B Squadron he had under his command. These eight men, having completed their three-month tour of duty, were due to be relieved and so far at Mirbat they had passed a relatively uneventful time, training the local *firqat* and enduring just three short bombardments; but now, as their commander joined them on the roof, all thoughts of a peaceful return to Britain vanished in the desperate need to fight off the guerrilla attack. The gendarmerie patrol had

Above: A member of the *adoo*, armed with an AKM, stands watch on a hilltop. The *adoo* used mostly Soviet-made weapons, supplied by the government of South Yemen. For close support their weapons were mainly portable Soviet equipment, such as RPG-7 rocket launchers and 12.7mm heavy machine guns, but they possessed heavier equipment in the form of some 122mm Katyusha rocket launchers. They also made use of material from the West when they could get it, as the deployment of a Carl Gustav rocket launcher at Mirbat demonstrated.

Left: Two Land Rovers meet in Dhofar. The one in the foreground carries an SAS patrol, whose leader confers with a member of the *firqat* patrol in the other vehicle.

Below: A Land Rover patrol of the Sultan's Armed Forces (SAF) man a Browning M2 0.5in heavy machine gun. The SAF comprised soldiers from many countries, including Britain, Pakistan, and Oman itself. In combination with the SAS and contingents from Iran and Jordan it quelled the Dhofari rebellion.

given them a brief warning; now they had to make their expertise tell.

When Kealy reached the roof, the whole area around seemed full of noise, smoke, and pandemonium. Corporal Bob Bradshaw, whose calmness and shrewdness under fire was to be one of the most important assets of the defence, pointed out the direction from which enemy mortar shells were coming, and the lines along which the *adoo* themselves were advancing. The captain tried to take stock of the situation. He knew that 100yd to the northwest, near the sea, was the Wali Fort, held by about 30 askars (armed tribesmen) from northern Oman. They were returning guerrilla fire, but were armed with rather dated .303in rifles, hardly a match at close quarters for the Soviet-made Kalashnikov assault rifles that the *adoo* were carrying. About 700yd to the northeast lay a larger fort held by about 25 more gendarmes. They too were returning enemy fire. In a gun-pit beside this Gendarmerie Fort was a World War II vintage 25pdr, manned by an Omani gunner. One of the SAS team, Trooper Labalaba, a Fijian, had already gone across to assist him. It was clear that the *firqat* in the town itself, weakened by the earlier dispatch of the patrol, would be of little immediate use as they struggled to organise themselves; nevertheless, given time, they might add their weight to the battle.

Around Kealy on the roof, and under heavy fire, Lance-Corporal Pete Wignall and Corporal Roger Chapman were in action with the two machine guns set up there – a GPMG and a heavy 0.5in Browning. Lance-Corporal Harris, meanwhile, was operating a mortar from a pit at the foot of the Batthouse.

The key to the action was the Gendarmerie Fort and the 25pdr pit. If that fell, then further resistance would be futile

All in all, these seemed puny defences against the weight of firepower that the guerrillas were deploying. But it was obvious that the key to the action would be the Gendarmerie Fort, and in particular the 25pdr pit. If that position fell, then further resistance would be futile. But if it could be held, then there was hope that help, in particular in the form of air support, might eventually arrive.

Over the gunfire Kealy heard from the other Fijian trooper, Savesaki, who was manning the short-range radio, that Labalaba at the fort had been shot in the chin. The captain agreed to Savesaki's request to take medical aid to him. This involved a run of 700yd over open ground but Savesaki, a top-class rugby player, set off confidently, weaving through the hail of bullets that seemed to bar his way. To the relief of those on the Batthouse roof, he fell panting and unharmed into the gun-pit. The 25pdr continued to fire.

The relief of the SAS men was short-lived, for their attention was suddenly taken from this act of considerable heroism by groups of well-armed rebels seen advancing towards the perimeter wire that defended the encampment on three sides. The *adoo* opened up with automatic weapons and their support weapons concentrated on the Gendarmerie Fort with devastating effect. Now the technical expertise of the SAS came into play. From the Batthouse, Wignall and Chapman laid down a murderous pattern of fire on the advancing guerrillas, firing furiously and accurately as they screamed for more ammunition, while their gun barrels steamed in the early morning drizzle. The *adoo* managed to reach the wire in considerable numbers, but to cross barbed wire is difficult, and the guerrillas had nothing more than their bodies or a blanket to throw across. They were now extremely vulnerable. Bradshaw was able to pick them off with his SLR as they became entangled in the wire; in particular he cut down one officer who was bravely urging on his men while astride the wire himself. But still some got through, and made for the fort.

With the clouds so low, there was little chance of the Strikemasters managing an attack for some time

---

What Kealy needed now was reinforcements and support. During the confusion he had almost forgotten the long-range radio. He called headquarters in Salalah for a helicopter to casevac Labalaba and for jets to attack the advancing rebels, but with the clouds still so low he realised there was little chance of the Strikemasters managing an attack for some time.

In spite of the great bravery shown by the *adoo*, and in

Below: An aerial photograph of an *adoo* encampment in Dhofar. The scrub vegetation gave good cover to ambush parties and also obscured movement across country.

Left: A trooper of 22 SAS in Oman during the 1970s. He wears olive-green fatigues and a jungle hat with the brim folded around the sides to form a peak at the front. On his belt is a water-bottle, ammunition pouch and an escape/evasion survival kit, and over his back a bergen rucksack is carried.

Instead of the standard British Army SLR (self-loading rifle) the trooper is armed with a US 5.56mm M16 rifle, a small-calibre automatic weapon with a maximum effective range of 400yd. The M16 is considerably lighter than the SLR (8.5lb to 11lb, loaded with 20-round magazines) and its full automatic capability makes it a useful weapon for close-quarters fighting.

Left: The roof of the Batthouse, the base of the SAS team stationed in Mirbat. It was from here that the SAS poured fire onto the rebel *adoo* advancing towards the perimeter wire. Two machine guns – a 7.62mm GPMG and a .50 calibre Browning – had been set up on the roof in sandbag emplacements.

Below: An SAS man throws a grenade. The fighting in Oman often took place at close-quarters on rock-strewn hillsides where grenades proved invaluable.

Left: During the battle of Mirbat much of the fighting revolved around the 25pdr gun-howitzer emplaced near the Gendarmerie Fort. At this time, the artillery arm of the SAF was equipped with weapons dating from World War II. These came in two types: the 5.5in gun and the 25pdr. The 25pdr had a long and successful career with both the British Army and many of the Commonwealth's forces. It entered service in 1939 and proved to be very versatile in action, serving as an anti-tank gun and, on a tank chassis, as a self-propelled artillery piece. The 25pdr is still in service with the SAF, but it is now supplemented by 105mm pack howitzers.
Below left: The Batthouse seen from the pit in which Lance-Corporal Harris manned the mortar. The close-quarters fighting of the battle of Mirbat meant that the mortar could not operate effectively, and Harris was forced to hold it against his chest in an attempt to get the range.

spite of the damage done to the Gendarmerie Fort by the bombardment, it was clear after about 0700 hours that the first crisis had passed. The initial assault had been held by a combination of physical courage (Savesaki's dash to the gun-pit) and solid experience, notably Bradshaw's efficient direction of the mortar and machine-gun fire that had chopped away at the guerrilla advance.

The SAS were still in grave danger, however. The main anxiety now was that the gun-pit was not responding to repeated radio calls. Kealy told Bradshaw to take command at the Batthouse, while the captain and Trooper Tobin investigated the situation in the gun-pit. As Kealy was about to set out, Bradshaw, smiling, pointed out that he still had his flip-flops on – in the excitement he had forgotten to change out of them. The rather embarrassed young captain went back to his room for his boots.

Kealy and Tobin, taking a less direct route than Savesaki, stealthily began their approach along a shallow wadi at the back of the Batthouse. However, as so often in war, strange, almost humorous events ran parallel to extreme peril. Kealy and Tobin, intent on their task, had to pass a laundry house. As they did so, an old man came out and insisted on shaking hands. The two SAS men stayed for a moment to exchange civilities before continuing. But now they had to race for the gun-pit under fire, covering each other as they went. Tobin reached the pit safely while Kealy took refuge in a nearby ammunition bay. Tobin immediately applied a drip to the

Below: An SAS sniper takes aim with his 7.62mm L42A1 rifle. The L42A1 is a .303in Lee-Enfield converted to standard Nato calibre and fitted with a sighting telescope.

adly wounded Omani gunner as Labalaba painfully crawled towards Kealy to explain that Savesaki, although adly wounded in the back, was covering the left-hand side f the fort.

Suddenly, there was an almighty explosion. Through the moke, Savesaki called to Kealy that more rebels had penetrated the wire and were heading towards them. The ttack was on again with a vengeance, and the second crisis f the battle of Mirbat had arrived.

Labalaba, in spite of his wounds, continued to man the 5pdr. He fired one shell at the *adoo,* reached down for nother which he put in the breech; but he was never able to use this round, for he was killed instantly by a bullet. Kealy's position was now under intense fire. The captain shot down ne eager rebel who had appeared round the corner of the ort, at point blank range, and was delighted to see that Tobin had taken over the 25pdr and was firing away. Delight was hort-lived, however, as Tobin in turn was shot – mortally wounded as it later turned out.

The nine members of the SAS at Mirbat upheld the traditions of the regiment in exemplary style. Captain Kealy (above), awarded the DSO for his part in the battle, had never been in action before. His bravery was matched by his ability to 'read' what was happening around him. Tragically, Kealy died on exercise in the Brecon Beacons in 1979.

Kealy spotted a grenade rolling slowly over the lip of the gun-pit. He braced himself for his last moment

---

Kealy radioed back to the Batthouse for Bradshaw to bring down mortar and machine-gun fire on the enemy who were now closing on the fort in consider-able numbers. Calm as ever, the corporal directed the machine-gun support, and assured Kealy that jets were on their way. Mortar support

was more difficult – the range was just too short, and Lance-Corporal Harris had to clutch the mortar tube to his chest in an effort to lay down effective fire. Kealy's elation at the news of air support was cut short when he spotted a grenade rolling slowly over the lip of the gun-pit. He braced himself for what he anticipated would be his last moment. But, to his disbelief, ike an ill-packed firework, the grenade failed to explode. Moments later Strikemaster jets of the SAF, with cannon iring, screamed in at low level to attack the rebels.

Under this air attack, the *adoo* began to pull back, and once again SAS expertise made itself felt, as Kealy from the ort and Bradshaw from the Batthouse directed the air strikes nto the most important areas, to inflict maximum damage on he enemy. Another set of air strikes at about 0915, concen-rating on the *adoo* heavy support weapons on the Jebel Ali, urthered hampered the attackers and by now, too, those members of the *firqat* who had remained in the town were in ction against the guerrillas who had moved to the southeast f the town.

The situation was still serious; only the air strikes, which had been carried out at very low altitude and at great risk to he pilots, had prevented the second major assault from arrying the day. But now, however, support in the form of resh troops arrived. As luck would have it, 23 members of G

Corporal Bradshaw, awarded the MM, was calmness and efficiency personified, directing support and interdiction fire from the Batthouse. Trooper Tobin, who courageously assisted Kealy in the defence of the gun-pit, was awarded a posthumous DCM, while Trooper Labalaba, also killed in defence of the gun-pit, received a posthumous Mention in Despatches.

Of the other members of the team, Trooper Savesaki made the dash under fire to keep the 25pdr in action; Lance-Corporal Harris continued to provide mortar support in spite of dangerously short ranges; Lance-Corporal Wignall and Corporal Reynolds provided support from the roof of the Batthouse; while Corporal Chapman played a key role by guiding in the first Strikemaster jets against the guerrillas.

Above: Sultan Qaboos bin Said, who seized power in Oman in 1970 by overthrowing his father. He requested aid from Britain when he realised that his armed forces were losing the war in Dhofar. The SAS, in the shape of British Army Training Teams, arrived in 1970, and six years later the insurgency had been brought to an end.

Squadron, 22 SAS (a squadron formed in 1966 as a result of the SAS's successes in Borneo) had landed in Oman only 24 hours before and were about to move to the hills for acclimatisation training when they were alerted to the situation at Mirbat. They flew by helicopter from Salalah to the seashore south-east of Mirbat and joined the intense battle. The rebels were amazed at the ferocity of the new attack (the reinforcements were few in number, but carried nine GPMGs between them), and began to pull back. Mirbat was relieved.

The SAS lost two men at Mirbat – Trooper Labalaba and Trooper Tobin who later died of wounds – and suffered two seriously wounded. Over 30 guerrilla dead were found on the battlefield, but many more died later of their wounds. The action had been a triumph of courage and expertise against enormous odds, and in a very real sense marked a turning point in the war. Had Mirbat fallen, then the government's credibility would have collapsed; its successful defence proved the worth of Sultan Qaboos' policies, and led to vicious arguments within the guerrilla movement.

After Mirbat, SAS teams in Dhofar continued their work of training *firqat* and taking the fight against the guerrillas into the mountains. Dealing with the *firqat* was never easy and there were many criticisms of the system. But the gradual erosion of support for the guerrillas among the population would certainly have taken longer without the SAS-led *firqat*, and it was the success of the 'hearts and minds' programme spearheaded by the SAS that underpinned the drive west as government forces gradually took the initiative.

SAS numbers in Dhofar were always small – often under 50 men and rarely over 100 – and, in comparison with the 15,000 or so troops (including contingents from Jordan and Iran) that took part in the offensives of 1974 and 1975, SAS involvement may therefore seem puny. But the role of the Special Air Service Regiment was to act as a backbone, a stiffening, for much larger forces; and in this they were invaluable. Whenever the going got tough they could be relied upon to provide all support necessary – as in January 1975, for example, in the attack on the guerrilla supply dump at Shershitti, when SAF troops caught in an ambush were relieved by SAS teams after three days' hard fighting.

The war in Dhofar came to a practical end after the SAF won an unexpectedly easy victory at Sarfait in October 1975 and took the Darra ridge in December of that year; by March 1976, the People's Democratic Republic of Yemen had come to an agreement with the Sultanate of Oman, and the Dhofar rebels were deprived of the safe haven and automatic re-supply that had been essential to their earlier success. There were still some isolated incidents, but the last SAS personnel left late in 1976. Since the arrival of units of the regiment in 1970, they had lost just 12 men killed, including the two who had died at Mirbat – the battle in which a 23-year-old captain and eight men had held off 250 heavily armed guerrillas.

5

SAS SIEGEBREAKERS
The Iranian Embassy

Page 69: Armed with a 'Hockler', a Heckler and Koch MP5A3 sub-machine gun, an SAS man springs across the embassy balcony. Above: 1250 hours on 2 May 1980, the third day of the siege. A brief glimpse of one of the gunmen as he appeared at the front door of the embassy to pick up a package of food. Negotiations had not yet broken down and a kind of flippancy was prevalent; the terrorists even complimented the police on the quality of meals they were sending in.

NUMBER 16 Princes Gate, former home of the Iranian embassy, stands overlooking the peaceful green expanse of Kensington Gardens in the heart of London's fashionable SW7. Today the house, once the scene of the busy comings and goings of the diplomatic community, stands empty, its doors chained and secured with a heavy padlock. On the first floor the elegant facade is crumbling and charred – the only remaining visible evidence of the events of 5 May 1980. In the early evening of that Bank Holiday Monday, several crashing explosions and the sharp crackle of automatic fire resounded along the terrace of houses at the climax of a tense siege which had kept the British government, its security forces and the public on tenterhooks for five days.

It was immediately supposed that the gunmen inside were blowing up the embassy, and slaughtering the hostages they had taken. Moments later, however, several dark silhouettes plunged into view. Vaulting agilely over the balcony from the house next door, they blasted their way through the window of the embassy with explosives. A pall of smoke belched from the shattered window, and the mysterious figures, dressed from head to toe in black, slipped inside. For the astonished onlookers at the front of the building, this was their first, and most likely their last, view of one of Britain's most secretive and specialised crack units going into action – the 22nd Special Air Service Regiment.

Will they really kill their hostages if their demands are not met?

The handling of sieges where hostages have been taken can never be a textbook operation. In every case hundreds of different factors have to be taken into account: who are the gunmen, what do they want, and will they really kill their hostages if their demands are not met? In many cases security forces have painstakingly negotiated a peaceful outcome, and a basic pattern of siege handling has been developed over the years. The provision of food, cigarettes, medical supplies and access to the media for the release of ideological statements are the results of hard bargaining. The position of the security forces is that they will never give anything away without getting something back in return - usually the release of a hostage. The question of a full-frontal assault by the police or army is never far from the minds of both security forces and the gunmen, but in recent years both parties have been haunted by the Munich massacre of 1972. Then, the German police attacked the terrorists on an airfield runway and the hostages, nine Israeli athletes, were killed by their Palestinian captors.

British security forces, however, have a first-rate record in the business of dealing with terrorist groups. The Spaghetti House restaurant siege of 1975 was ended without casualties, and, later that year, IRA gunmen gave themselves up in a flat in Balcombe Street, London, without harming a middle-aged couple they had taken hostage. In the latter siege, mention, on the BBC, of the SAS being in the vicinity was

BATTLEDRESS AND WEAPONS

The 22nd SAS Regiment, unlike most units of the regular British Army, allows its men a degree of personal choice in both the weapons and clothing used on active service.

At the embassy the need was for light, comfortable clothing that would not interfere with movement. The men wore tight-fitting black combat clothing with high patrol boots and 'Northern Ireland' gloves, and a black-covered flak vest covered the torso. Headwear consisted of a standard-issue army respirator and a grey anti-flash hood – both helped to reduce the effects of smoke and heat generated by explosions.

A black belt held an open-top holster for the 9mm Browning automatic pistol and a series of pouches that contained magnesium-based stun-grenades and 30-round magazines for the Heckler and Koch sub-machine gun.

The 9mm Heckler and Koch MP5A3 was perhaps the most effective part of the SAS arsenal deployed at Princes Gate. Of West German origin, it was pressed into service after two SAS men had witnessed its effectiveness in close-quarters combat during the GSG9 assault on an airliner at Mogadishu. The 'Hockler', as the MP5A3 is known to the SAS, is light (4.4lb), short (12.8in) and can fire at a rate of up to 650rpm or, if need be, single shots to take out individual targets.

Above: The Heckler and Koch MP5A3 sub-machine gun (top) and the 9mm Browning HP automatic pistol. (Weapons not shown to scale.)

believed to have brought the terrorists out. But the situation at Princes Gate proved far more complex.

At 1132 hours on the morning of Wednesday 30 April, a group of unidentified gunmen had burst in through the front doors of the embassy after spraying the outer glass door with bullets. The terrified occupants of the five-story building were quickly rounded up – in addition to the 19 Iranians in the embassy there were seven non-Iranians, including two men from the BBC and Police Constable Trevor Lock from Scotland Yard's Diplomatic Protection Group.

Surveillance equipment monitored everything that went on

With sirens blaring and lights flashing, police units were on the scene within minutes – Lock had succeeded in transmitting an emergency signal through to the Yard before being overpowered by the raiders. They were soon joined by the more specialist units at Scotland Yard's disposal: D11, known as the 'Blue Berets', an elite unit of police marksmen, took up positions around the building, followed by C13, the anti-terrorist squad, while the Special Patrol Group and members of C7, the Yard's Technical Support Branch, were also quickly on the scene. The latter were in charge of the surveillance equipment that monitored everything that went on inside the embassy. By mid-afternoon plainclothes SAS men were also present – their arrival, however, was considerably more discreet.

With the embassy effectively sealed off and surrounded, the police received the gunmen's demands over the telephone at 1435. The gunmen identified themselves as the Group of the Martyr. In opposition to the harsh Islamic Iranian regime of the Ayatollah Khomeini, they were fighting for the liberation of Khuzestan, an oil-rich district inhabited by Arabs in the southwest of Iran, that had a history of revolt against Iranian domination. Their demands included the release of 91 Arab prisoners held in Iran, their immediate transfer from gaol to London, and a request for Arab ambassadors to mediate with the British authorities. Noon the next day was the deadline – if it was not met they would blow up the embassy and execute the hostages.

In Zulu Control, the main police headquarters set up further down the terrace, the Yard mulled over the immediate problems of the situation. In both the Spaghetti House and Balcombe Street sieges background knowledge of the men involved had proved invaluable in wearing them down. The police, however, knew little of the Group of the Martyr, and, as far as they could see, only one of the gunmen could speak English. The police were also unaware of how many hostages had been taken, and, although they soon discovered there were 26, held by six terrorists, it was difficult to fix their location in the rambling building. The authorities began their tense negotiations almost immediately, adopting the tried and tested 'softly-softly' approach.

Meanwhile the SAS were making their own preparations

1 Microphones and surveillan[ce] devices are lowered down the chimney to monitor the movements of the terrorists a[nd] hostages inside the embassy.

2 An SAS assault force abseil[s] down from the roof in pairs. On the way down a flailing bo[dy] breaks a back window and the element of surprise is almost [lost]. One of the team becomes entangled in a descent rope, making it impossible to use fra[me] charges. They hack their way through the strengthened-glas[s] windows on the first and gro[und] floors and toss in a stun-grena[de]. Entering the building, they sho[ot] a gunman in the front hallway a[nd] race towards the telex room.

3 Members of the frontal-assa[ult] group blast their way through first-floor windows with fram[e] charges and lob in a stun-gren[ade]. Reaching the telex room, the[y] burst in and shoot two terror[ists] dead.

sault on the Iranian embassy

telex room

first-floor landing

front hallway

to deal with the situation. At a barracks in Regent's Park a scale model of the besieged embassy had been constructed, to familiarise the men with every detail of the layout of the building they would have to assault if police negotiations broke down.

Operation Nimrod, as it became known, was nothing new to the SAS. Since the early 1970s, SAS training procedures had placed great emphasis on the fight against international terrorism. At Bradbury Lines, the SAS headquarters at Hereford, a close-quarter battle (CQB) house has been constructed for the purpose of training troopers in the use of smallarms in enclosed spaces. In the CQB house, SAS men sit in a room with a number of 'terrorist' straw dummies while their colleagues storm in and riddle the dummies with live ammunition from their silenced Sterling sub-machine guns and Browning automatics. It is not an exercise where mistakes can be made. Lightning reflexes, and the ability to shoot accurately and lethally while running, crouching or rolling across the floor, are the keys to such combat skills.

Their marksmanship is only part of the story, however. First of all, the SAS have to get into the area where the hostages are being held. While SAS training involves stretching a man's resources and endurance to the limits, it also teaches him all the basic assault techniques, including abseiling – part of the mountain-training programme – and the use of explosives to blast a way into sealed buildings.

Equipment, specially developed for these particularly hazardous operations, is also crucial to their success. For example, 'frame charges' were used to break through the strengthened glass of the embassy's windows. These are large rectangles of plastic explosive that are placed flush against the glass, so that the whole window is blown in when the charges are detonated.

Next, 'stun-grenades' were thrown in. The stun-grenade had been specially developed by the SAS for just such an operation as Nimrod. When detonated, it produces a blinding flash, a deafening bang and a cloud of smoke. It is in the moment after the explosion, when gunmen are temporarily blinded and disorientated by the smoke and the noise, that the SAS man must act. These grenades had been supplied by the SAS to the German GSG9 anti-terrorist unit, were used successfully in an assault on a hijacked Lufthansa aircraft on the runway at Mogadishu in Somalia in 1977, and were perfectly suited to the Princes Gate operation.

To assist in the assault, preparations were also being made at the embassy itself. In order to determine the exact position of the gunmen, Scotland Yard's C7 installed a number of microphones and surveillance devices in the chimneys and walls of adjoining buildings. To cover the noise of this installation work, a barrage of road drills was set up in nearby Ennismore Gardens – the Gas Board was supposedly carrying out emergency repairs after the report

Above: A series of photographs showing the sequence of events as SAS teams moved into the embassy. From left to right: covered by police snipers, SAS men lay frame charges on a window frame; these explode; the SAS men enter the building; the curtains burst into flame, a fire which eventually spread to the entire building.

Far left: Police Constable Trevor Lock with Mustapha Karkouti, a Lebanese journalist, speaking to the police on the terrorists' behalf. The Iranians spoke little English, so hostages were used to relay their demands. Lock later helped the SAS to release the hostages by grappling with the terrorists' leader.

75

Beginning in the 1960s, political and paramilitary liberation groups began to pursue their aims with attacks that would attract widespread public attention. One popular method was to hijack airliners, notable examples being the Dawson's Field hijack in 1970, Entebbe in 1976 and Mogadishu in 1977 (where two SAS men helped the West German GSG9 counter-terrorist unit). The kidnapping of the OPEC oil ministers in 1975 and the seizure of a Dutch train and the Indonesian consulate in Amsterdam by South Moluccan nationalists in December 1975 are other examples of the sort of high-profile targets that focused the attention of the world on terrorists and their causes. The governments of the United States and western Europe did not welcome these developments as terrorist violence was largely directed against their citizens. They began to allocate resources to units which would use force to end terrorist situations when negotiations had failed. In Britain, the SAS undertook to fulfil this role on the army's behalf. The willingness to use such units, together with the exchange of intelligence and experience amongst the security services of the United States and western Europe, has given governments an effective ability to respond to terrorist incidents.

of a gas leak in the street. Unknown to the gunmen inside, a section of wall between the embassy and the house next door was also being removed. As quietly as possible the bricks were removed one by one, leaving only a thin sheet of plaster for an assault team to kick their way through.

Outside in the street things were not going so well. Patient negotiations on the part of the police had secured the release of several hostages, food and cigarettes had been passed in to the gunmen, and two deadlines had passed without incident. By the evening of 1 May, the second day of the siege, the gunmen had discarded their demand for the release of the 91 prisoners in Iran, hoping that, through the mediation of the requested Arab ambassadors, they could negotiate a safe passage out of the country. The British government, however, was taking a firm stand on the questions of mediation and safe conduct, and, to the fury of the gunmen, radio news had made no mention whatsoever of their demand for Arab mediators. Frustrated and jumpy, the gunmen threatened to kill hostages unless their demands were broadcast in full. For several tense minutes they sat listening to Capital Radio's nine o'clock news bulletin. The demand for the mediators was stated and the crisis was temporarily averted, but the mediators failed to materialise.

By the morning of the sixth day, Monday 5 May, the

situation was deteriorating rapidly. With the government refusing to make any concessions, the police had little bargaining power left, and had lost the precious confidence of the terrorists. Inside the building, the strain of the past days was beginning to tell. The gunmen had grown pessimistic of their chances of escape, and a raging political argument, which had broken out between them and several of the Iranian hostages the night before, brought the situation to the brink of catastrophe. At 1140 hours, Constable Lock appeared at the window to say that his captors would start shooting the hostages unless news of the Arab mediators was immediately forthcoming. Desperately playing for time, the police persuaded the gunmen to wait until the midday BBC news. The BBC bulletin, however, made little impression on the gunmen and at 1331 three shots were heard from inside the embassy. The time for a 'softly-softly' approach was over.

After restating their demands, three more shots were heard

For the gunmen, surrender was now the only realistic way out, but at 1850, after having restated their demands, three more shots were heard and the dead body of the embassy press officer was pushed out of the front door onto the pavement. The police responded at once. Seemingly giving in to their demands, the negotiators made contact with the leader of the gunmen, offered him safe conduct and an aircraft to take the group out of the country. But as the terrorist leader discussed the details of the bus to the airport he was also giving away his position to the waiting SAS.

Far left: Two SAS men in plainclothes and with their faces obscured by balaclavas cover the front of the embassy with pistols. Below: Sim Harris, a BBC journalist who happened to be at the embassy at the time of the terrorist takeover, escapes from the burning building. An SAS man with a Heckler and Koch covers him.

Above: The bodies of the terrorists were removed from the burnt-out embassy on 7 May by firemen. Here a corpse, wrapped in a body bag, is lowered from the second-floor front window of the embassy.

At 1923, the black-clad assault team crashed into the embassy. Their faces masked with respirators, the SAS men stormed the building from three sides. The initial assault came from the back. Abseiling down ropes from the roof, the first pair reached the terrace at the back of the embassy, but were unable to detonate their frame charges because of a colleague entangled in a rope above them. A second pair dropped to the first-floor back balcony and both teams were forced to hack their way in through bullet-proof glass. A stun-grenade was thrown in and the SAS made for the telex room on the second floor where they knew, from the C7 surveillance, that a number of the hostages were being held.

On the first-floor landing the terrorist leader was with Trevor Lock, and as an SAS man appeared at the window he raised his gun to fire. Lock sprang into action, hurling himself at the gunman and grappling with him until the SAS man was able to shoot him. Meanwhile at the front of the building, in full view of the TV cameras, the SAS blasted through the first-floor window and lobbed in a stun-grenade. Flames poured from the window, and out of the thick smoke came the first of the hostages, the BBC man Sim Harris, into the welcoming hands of an SAS trooper. A third team stormed through the thin sheets of plaster where the bricks had been removed.

Racing through the burning building, the SAS converged on the telex room. Hearing the mayhem of the assault, the gunman guarding the hostages turned his gun onto them – killing one and wounding two others. When the SAS burst in, he and two colleagues had mingled with the hostages scattered around the floor of the room. The rescuers demanded to know which ones were the terrorists. As they were pointed out the SAS shot two of them dead. Several of the hostages interviewed afterwards said that the gunmen tried to surrender, but, in the heat of the battle, amid the smoke and confusion and wailing of the hostages, the SAS took what action was deemed necessary.

In the wake of the assault the bodies of five of the six gunmen were carried out of the embassy; two were taken from the telex room, one from an office at the back, one from the embassy hallway near the front door and the fifth from the first floor. All had died from firearm wounds to the head and chest. As for the SAS, they suffered no casualties and left the area in two Avis vans.

The Iranian embassy siege gripped the nation's imagination for six long days and, thanks to television, everyone in the country had a grandstand view of the unfolding drama. It was on this dangerous and dramatic stage that the SAS made their public debut. Negotiation by the police kept the hostages alive, but it was the SAS, in a brief 17-minute exchange, who brought them freedom. The operation at Princes Gate was carried out with almost surgical precision, and, although the gunmen killed one of the hostages in the final shoot-out, SAS training in anti-terrorist techniques was shown to be second to none.

6

A NEW BATTLEFIELD
The Falklands War

Disputes about the ownership of the Falkland Islands (known to Argentina as the Malvinas) date back to 1770, when Britain, France and Spain nearly went to war over the matter. At this time Britain accepted Spain's right to part of the islands, and in 1790 renounced any colonial ambitions in South America. Authority over the islands passed to Argentina in 1820 despite the British consul's protests. The United States became involved when an American sealing ship, the *Harriet*, was detained and its cargo impounded by the Argentinian governor of the islands. An American warship then wrecked the Argentinian settlement in retaliation, and its captain declared the islands free of all government.

Britain occupied the islands in 1833, and the matter of ownership seemed settled. But Argentina never accepted Britain's claim, and generations of Argentinian children were taught in school that the islands belonged to their country. In early 1982, when the authoritarian junta in power in Argentina found itself increasingly unpopular, it seized on the Malvinas issue as a means to gain public support. On 2 April 1982, Argentina invaded the Falklands, defeating the small British garrison there.

THE SAS deployed no less than one and a half of its four squadrons during operations to re-take the Falklands. Their tasks included the traditional strategic ones of infiltration for surveillance and intelligence-gathering, together with tactical ones concerned with diversionary attacks and seizing key features in front of the main attacking force. Moreover they did once again what David Stirling and his original 'L' Detachment had done some 40 years earlier – mounted raids to destroy enemy aircraft on their airfields.

The first job which D Squadron undertook was part of Operation Paraquat, the recapture of South Georgia, and as the Task Force commander, Rear Admiral John 'Sandy' Woodward, required information about enemy dispositions at Leith and Grytviken in order to plan his attack, D Squadron was invited to find out about Leith. It was getting ashore that was to prove the most hazardous undertaking. Initial attempts to insert observation posts on 21 April resulted in two Wessex helicopters crashing because of extremely poor weather. Later the SAS managed to get ashore by Gemini landing craft. There was not a great deal of fighting to do, for the Argentinians had been persuaded by the effective use of naval gunfire support, directed by a Forward Observation Officer, that British intentions were serious. But there were some lively incidents, as Corporal Davey of 19 Troop reported, during the advance on Grytviken:

'In the area where the Brown Mountain ridge line joined the coast we saw what appeared to be men in brown balaclavas among the tussock grass. They were engaged by GPMG fire from approximately 800 metres and by

naval gunfire. Captain Hamilton and I also engaged a possible enemy position on the top of Brown Mountain with Milan [anti-tank missile]. Advancing across open ground towards the ridge line we discovered that the balaclava'd enemy were in fact seven or eight elephant seals, which were now somewhat the worse for wear! The enemy position on Brown Mountain had been a piece of angle iron on which we had scored a direct hit.'

Soon after this, on 25 April, the SAS, together with Royal Marines, accepted the surrender of the Argentinian garrison at Grytviken. Next day the remaining enemy troops at Leith surrendered to the SAS. All this would have been relatively straightforward, had it not been for the exceptionally difficult weather. However, the SAS's major contribution to re-taking the Falklands was still to come.

An enemy patrol was quickly silenced by automatic fire

On 1 May, almost exactly a month after Argentina invaded, the first surveillance patrols of G Squadron were landed by helicopter on East Falkland. For nearly three weeks they stayed close to enemy positions, observing and reporting, and so provided the vital information which enabled the Task Force to make the landings at San Carlos, the key operation leading to total victory. On 14 May, about a week before the main landings, D Squadron, fresh from their success in South Georgia, were committed to a classic SAS-type raid on the airfield at Pebble Island. This involved a 45-minute flight by three Sea Kings from HMS *Hermes*, followed by a 4-mile walk from the Landing Zone to a secure base, then on a further 2½ miles to the airstrip. Supported by naval gunfire and illuminating rounds, the raiders shot up the aircraft with smallarms and rockets, despite some enemy fire and a land mine which blew one SAS man some 10ft backwards, but without injuring him too badly. An enemy patrol was nearby during their return journey, but was

Page 79: Dawn on the Falkland Islands.

Far left: The Argentinian submarine *Santa Fe* lies damaged in the harbour at Grytviken on South Georgia. During Operation Paraquat (the recapture of South Georgia), D Squadron of the SAS played an important role. The first stage of the mission was to carry out a reconnaissance for the main landing by the Royal Marines. Three patrols of D Squadron's Mountain Troop landed on Fortuna Glacier on 21 April, but blizzards and gales prevented them from moving. During attempts to extract them, two Wessex Helicopters crashed (above). Lieutenant-Commander Ian Stanley won a Distinguished Service Order when he flew the patrols out on 22 April in an overloaded Wessex Mk 3 helicopter. D Squadron's Boat Troop also got into trouble on 23 April when two of their five boats suffered engine failures and threatened to drift into the Antarctic before being rescued.

quickly silenced by automatic fire. Mission completed, the raiders all flew back to *Hermes* having destroyed 11 enemy aircraft and a considerable amount of enemy ammunition and explosives supplies.

Soon after this there was a tragic accident. During a cross-decking from *Hermes* to *Intrepid* a Sea King helicopter with 27 passengers and three crew crashed into the sea, probably caused by an albatross flying into the engine intake. Eighteen men of D and G Squadrons were lost. Yet even this tragedy did not prevent the SAS continuing with their vital duties. As the CO of 22 SAS, Lieutenant-Colonel Michael Rose, wrote at the time: 'The Regiment has taken it well and are getting on with the fighting at present.' But he added that he would be happy when all his men were ashore, their lives in their own hands. D Squadron still had plenty to do. They covered the main landings by diversionary attacks at Darwin and Goose Green. After the main landing had been successful, they inserted a patrol at Mount Kent and subsequently reinforced it, an action which proved of vital importance in the subsequent advance to Port Stanley. They also ambushed enemy patrols, carried out raids, gathered information about Argentinian positions and strengths, mounted operations on West Falkland, and helped in the final capture of Port Stanley with further harassing and diversionary attacks. It was all in the best SAS traditions of daring, versatility, discipline, initiative and

Below: The remnants of an Argentinian Pucará, blown up during the SAS raid on Pebble Island during the night of 14/15 May. The first stage of this operation was the landing of an eight-man SAS reconnaissance team on the night of 11/12 May. They reported back on the strength of the Argentinian forces. Then on 14 May 45 men from D Squadron, plus a naval gunfire support team, were landed by helicopter. While ships offshore shelled Argentinian positions, the SAS men placed demolition charges that destroyed 11 aircraft. One SAS officer referred to it as 'the kind of thing we have not had the chance to do since World War II'.

Right: A Fijian NCO of 22 SAS during the Falklands campaign. He wears a civilian Gove-Tex weatherproof jacket to protect him against the cold wind and dampness of the islands. Under the jacket he wears the popular 'woolly-pully' sweater and Royal Marine DPM trousers. His belt order uses both British and US equipment. The belt is the US M56, with a US ammunition pouch for an M16 to the left of the buckle. By his left arm is a British 1944-pattern water-bottle carrier used as a pouch, while on the right he has a 1944-pattern compass pouch. He is armed with a camouflaged 7.62mm self-loading rifle.

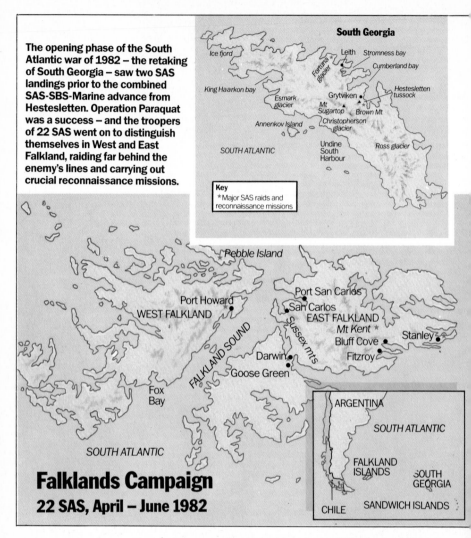

The opening phase of the South Atlantic war of 1982 – the retaking of South Georgia – saw two SAS landings prior to the combined SAS-SBS-Marine advance from Hestesletten. Operation Paraquat was a success – and the troopers of 22 SAS went on to distinguish themselves in West and East Falkland, raiding far behind the enemy's lines and carrying out crucial reconnaissance missions.

South Georgia

Ice fjord
Leith
Stromness bay
Fortuna glacier
Cumberland bay
King Haarkon bay
Hestesletten tussock
Esmark glacier
Grytviken
Mt Sugartop
Brown Mt
Annenkov Island
Christopherson glacier
SOUTH ATLANTIC
Undine South Harbour
Ross glacier

Key
* Major SAS raids and reconnaissance missions

Pebble Island
Port San Carlos
Port Howard
San Carlos
WEST FALKLAND
EAST FALKLAND
Mt Kent *
Stanley
Bluff Cove
Sussex mts
FALKLAND SOUND
Darwin
Fitzroy
Goose Green
Fox Bay
ARGENTINA
SOUTH ATLANTIC
SOUTH ATLANTIC
FALKLAND ISLANDS
SOUTH GEORGIA
CHILE
SANDWICH ISLANDS

Falklands Campaign
22 SAS, April – June 1982

determination in the face of setbacks and losses. It was a further demonstration of what could be gained from the imaginative, bold and skilful use of small numbers.

Meanwhile, G Squadron was just as busy on intelligence-gathering duties. One of the citations for a gallantry award for the commander of a four-man patrol gives an impression of one such mission:

'Inserted by helicopter on to East Falkland from HMS *Hermes* at a range of 120 miles, he positioned his patrol in close proximity to enemy positions, cut off from any form of rescue should he have been compromised. This position he maintained for a period of 26 days. During this time he produced a clear picture of enemy activity in the Stanley area, intelligence available from no other means, which has proved vital in the planning of the final assault.' The citation went on to explain how exemplary this patrol's reports had been. It enabled an air strike to be successfully directed against enemy helicopter concentrations, thus robbing them of their ability to re-deploy troops rapidly. Moreover, the conditions under which the patrol lived were frightful – freezing rain, gale-force winds, with little or no cover either from the elements or from view, simply shallow holes scraped in the ground with camouflaged chicken wire to help hide them. In spite of this extreme vulnerability the patrol's intelligence reports were regular and detailed. 'In this respect,' concludes the citation, 'the endurance and fortitude of all his patrol was magnificent. By his personal example he set the highest standards which his patrol both admired and responded to in the most positive way. His actions, carried out in a totally hostile environment, were in the highest traditions of his Regiment.'

Accurate details of the enemy's guns, defences and aircraft were reported

All in all, G Squadron's surveillance operations were so successful that they were able to give a detailed picture of what the Argentinians were up to from the time they initially deployed on 1 May until final victory six weeks later. It was an exemplary illustration of living behind the enemy lines, under extremely uncomfortable and hazardous conditions,

Below: An SAS trooper in the foreground trudges past four Scots Guardsmen on Goat ridge. SAS operations in the Falklands usually took place in no-man's-land. Their shadowy presence often went unnoticed by friend and foe alike.

often so close to enemy positions that accurate details of their guns, defences and aircraft could be reported. Such details, of course, enabled the British Task Force to subject the Argentinian positions to naval gunfire and air strikes, all part of the relentless pressure which in the end led the Argentinian commander to give up.

In war much depends on the personality and determination of the commanders concerned, and Lieutenant-Colonel Rose was convinced from the outset that the man leading 3 Commando Brigade, Brigadier Julian Thompson, would be the key figure in the land battle, particularly as many of his decisions would be influenced by the information gained by SAS patrols. It was therefore to Brigadier Thompson's headquarters that the CO of 22 SAS attached himself. The two of them agreed early on that some sort of psychological operations would be necessary, and after some false starts, Rose was able to persuade the demoralised Argentinians to consider surrender.

One of the first important steps was opening a line of communication to the Argentinian headquarters, which was done on 6 June. About a week later, Rose flew by helicopter to Port Stanley to see General Menéndez. It was soon plain that the past week of psychological persuasion – to the tune that further fighting was pointless, that the rift between Argentina and Britain would become unbridgeable, that the Argentinian Army would become known as the butchers of Port Stanley – had been effective. After some hours of negotiation, Menéndez agreed, and soon after that, on 14 June, General Jeremy Moore arrived to sign the official instrument of Argentinian surrender.

Below: Men of D Squadron, 22 SAS and 148 Naval Gunfire Observation Battery prepare equipment for helicopter transportation. An orange smoke flare signals their position to the incoming Sea King, while a man on the right gives visual signals.